2400

TANZANIA

An African Experiment

Profiles
NATIONS OF CONTEMPORARY AFRICA
Larry Bowman, Series Editor

Also of Interest

TANZANIA

An African Experiment

Rodger Yeager

Westview Press • Boulder, Colorado

Gower • Hampshire, England

Profiles/Nations of Contemporary Africa

Copyright © 1982 by Westview Press, Inc.

Published in 1982 in the United States of America by
  Westview Press, Inc.
  5500 Central Avenue
  Boulder, Colorado 80301
  Frederick A. Praeger, President and Publisher

Published in 1982 in Great Britain by
  Gower Publishing Company Limited
  Gower House, Croft Road
  Aldershot, Hants., GU11 3HR England

Library of Congress Cataloging in Publication Data
Yeager, Rodger.
  Tanzania, an African experiment.
  (Nations of contemporary Africa)
  Bibliography: p.
  Includes index.
  1. Tanzania. I. Title. II. Series.
DT438.Y4   1982   967.8   82-1965
ISBN 0-89158-923-6   AACR2

British Library Cataloguing in Publication Data
Yeager, Rodger
  Tanzania. — (Profiles, nations of contemporary Africa)
  1. Tanzania — History   I. Title   II. Series
  967'.8   DT444
ISBN 0-566-00554-9

Printed and bound in the United States of America

For Jan

Contents

Illustrations and Tables

Acknowledgments

Tanzania has influenced my life since 1964, when as a young graduate student I first arrived in the country to engage in local political research and to undertake a working assignment in the Ministry of Lands, Settlement, and Water Development. I cannot hope to acknowledge everyone who, over the years, has helped me to appreciate the full significance of Tanzania. For making it all possible, I must again thank my teacher and friend Fred G. Burke.

A number of Americans and Tanzanians have provided considerable assistance as I prepared this volume. Among the Americans, special thanks go to two non-Africanist colleagues in the West Virginia University Department of Political Science. Associate Chairman Allan Hammock released me from some of my normal academic duties and thereby gave me a fighting chance of meeting my externally mandated and self-inflicted deadlines. Another political scientist, Robert DiClerico, patiently responded to my pleas for stylistic advice, even though my frequent intrusions seemed always to tear him away from his own writing on the U.S. presidency. Robert Maxwell, former field director of the university's Tanzanian agricultural education projects, contributed valuable insights that reflected his many years of dedicated service in eastern Africa. Betty Maxwell, Bob's wife, typed the final manuscript and offered equally important comments on its content. I am also indebted to one of my graduate students, Terri Reidenour, who laboriously checked the chapter drafts for technical accuracy and readability.

My greatest appreciation is reserved for Norman Miller, an academic colleague of the first order and a friend to whom I owe much. Norman and I have taken many intellectual safaris together on both sides of the ocean, and he is writing the Kenya volume for the series in which this book appears. With Norman, Kenya is in good hands.

My most recent involvement with Tanzania has been through the Manpower Development Division of the Ministry of Agriculture. I want to express my gratitude to two former directors of the division, Henry Kasiga and John E. U. Mchechu, for their hospitality and willingness to discuss Tanzania's developmental problems. These and many other public servants have shown me the true meaning of the Tanzanian appellation *ndugu* (comrade). I am particularly obliged to the following development and training officers whom I came to know as students at West Virginia University: Martin Busanda, Vincent Hiza, Andrew Ibrahim, George Lulandala, Ildefons Lupanga, Joas Mannento, Johnson Mawalla, Betty Mlingi, Lily Mosha, Michael Mziray, Sylvia and Francis Shao, Ignas Swai, and the late Gabriel Kasenghwa. With the tragic exception of Ndugu Kasenghwa, these men and women provide living examples of the committed leadership envisioned by President Julius Nyerere. Associating with them has immensely heightened my sensitivity to the Tanzanian experiment and has enabled me to avoid several errors of fact and interpretation. Of course, I alone am responsible for any remaining inaccuracies and sins of poor judgment.

Rodger Yeager

Introduction

This book provides an overview of Tanzania, one of the economically poorest yet socially and politically most innovative countries in tropical Africa. This venture will carry us briefly into the rich Tanzanian past, which began with the dawn of humanity itself and includes contributions from many of the world's major cultures. The main focus, however, will be on the last twenty years. During this period Tanganyika and Zanzibar gained their independence and joined to form the United Republic of Tanzania.[1] The country then undertook an experiment in political and economic development that has provoked widely differing reactions.

On the one hand, Tanzania is viewed as a conspicuously successful new state whose leaders have been able to avoid the postindependence perils of neocolonialism, elitism, and governmental instability and instead to construct an order in which brave political slogans are becoming social and cultural realities. According to this view, Tanzania is one developing country where the present generation has a real chance of achieving *uhuru* ("freedom"), *umoja* ("unity"), *ujamaa* ("socialism"), and *maendeleo* ("development").

From another perspective the picture is less bright: Tanzania is also portrayed as a case study of misplaced philosophical idealism, lost developmental opportunities, and unfulfilled political promises. To the left, the country is a professed socialist state whose elites have abandoned true socialism. To the right, these same elites have failed to make the hard investment decisions that are a sine qua non of any successful transition to modernity.

One factor upon which critics and advocates can agree is the significance of Tanzania's top political leadership, and particularly that of President Julius Nyerere. More than anything else, his words and deeds are responsible for the passion with which Tanzania is both praised and condemned by those who have observed and participated in its national life. There is little disagreement about the moral content of Nyerere's thought and his vision of a just and prosperous society. The same cannot be said for the means selected and results obtained in pursuit of this dream. Perhaps because Nyerere has stimulated his people to aim at such an alluring yet elusive target, critics are especially enthusiastic when the shot approaches its mark and equally anxious when it misses.

The Tanzanian government is highly structured and is active at all levels.

1

Before independence, the mainland was a United Nations trust territory under British administration, and Zanzibar was a British protectorate. Since the early 1960s, these former colonial outposts have evolved into a single-party state with a powerful central apparatus controlled by the Chama cha Mapinduzi (Revolutionary party), and twenty-five regional centers of authority. Local politics and government are organized from the district level down to the individual household and workplace. Internationally, Tanzania remains adamantly non-aligned with any major power bloc but has consistently served as a leading "front-line" state in support of the southern African liberation struggle. Tanzanian armies also waged a unilateral war of liberation to free neighboring Uganda from the repressive rule of Idi Amin.

For all of the controversy surrounding its socioeconomic and political systems, in many respects Tanzania is not unlike other developing countries. Located between 2° and 10° south latitude and 30° to 40° east longitude, the country encompasses a total area of 945,262 square kilometers (378,105 square miles), including 60,000 square kilometers (24,000 square miles) of lakes and rivers. Topographically, coastal lowlands give way to a savanna that rises to 1,800 meters (5,940 feet) between two branches of eastern Africa's Great Rift Valley. Mountains and hilly highlands form natural boundaries in parts of the south, west, and north. The northern highlands are dominated by the tallest mountain in Africa, Kilimanjaro, which rises to 5,879 meters (19,340 feet).

The Tanzanian climate is influenced by two Indian Ocean monsoons, which in a good year will bring one short and one long rainy season. The rains are frequently unreliable, and most of the country is dry for a large part of the year. Temperature varies with altitude; average minimum readings for June and July are between 10° and 20°C. (50° to 68°F.) and average maxima during December and January are from 25° to 30.5°C. (77° to 87°F.).

Reflecting the uneven distribution of water, arable land, and economic opportunity, Tanzania's population is concentrated on Zanzibar and at the periphery of the mainland. The population has grown from about 12 million in 1967 to more than 18 million in 1981 and continues to increase at an average annual rate of more than 3 percent. Nearly 90 percent of all Tanzanians live in the rural areas. The Tanzanian population is made up of more than 120 ethnic groups. Most of these groups are small; the largest accounts for only 13 percent of the total population. Although each group has its own language or dialect, the coastal Kiswahili language serves as an effective lingua franca.

The cash economy is managed by the government, with considerable private involvement in small-scale productive activities. The agricultural sector employs more than 80 percent of the work force and emphasizes both commercial and subsistence crops. In recent years, low agricultural productivity, oscillating world commodity prices, and rising costs of petroleum and other imports have produced widening trade and balance-of-payments deficits. Tanzania is also heavily dependent on foreign aid and must even import food. The production and distribution of sufficient nutrients for a rapidly growing population are the country's most pressing developmental problem.

These facts should hold few surprises for even the most casual observer of

UNITED REPUBLIC OF TANZANIA

Africa and other developing areas. But on closer examination Tanzania is not so typical of poor countries. Under unusually imaginative political leadership, Tanzanians have transformed their human environment to present a model of modernizing achievement to some and a lesson in developmental failure to others. This study seeks to help the reader determine which is the more accurate picture of what must surely be one of Africa's most important and most controversial nations.

1

The Origins of Tanzania

PRECOLONIAL TANZANIA

Eastern Africa began preparing to receive human society during the Miocene epoch, about fifteen million years ago. Huge tectonic upheavals raised a forested upland by 900 meters (3,000 feet) and created the highlands of contemporary Ethiopia, Kenya, and mainland Tanzania. Under the force of this vertical thrust, volcanoes erupted and the earth's crust cracked and collapsed. Thus was formed the Great Rift Valley, which extends from north of the Gulf of Aqaba to south of the Zambezi River. As time passed, the volcanoes became inactive and most were weathered to less than one-tenth of their former size. The floor of the valley sank even lower, and many lakes were created, of which only a few remain along the eastern and western branches of the Rift. In Tanzania, these lakes include Natron, Eyasi, and Manyara in the east and Tanganyika, Rukwa, and Malawi to the west. Areas lying between the walls of the eastern and western Rift were cast under permanent rain shadows, depriving the tropical forests of essential water and providing conditions favorable to the savanna of grass and scattered trees that now predominates in central Tanzania. This savanna country became the scene of a crucial chapter in human evolution.

The Birthplace of Man

The Miocene was the age of the arboreal apes. These primates were heavily dependent on the trees for their food and shelter. As the forests receded, a small apelike hominid, *Ramapithecus*, became adapted to the wooded fringe. *Ramapithecus* eventually gravitated to the open country of the Great Rift Valley and there gave rise to still other hominids, including man.

The search for our evolutionary progenitors continues near the existing and extinct lakes of the Rift.[1] Tanzania is the scene of two pioneering discoveries in this quest, made by the remarkable team of prehistorians led by Louis and Mary Leakey. In 1959 Mary Leakey came upon the broken remains of a manlike hominid, *Zinjanthropus boisei* ("East African man"). The find was made at Olduvai Gorge, the site of a vanished lake on the edge of the Serengeti Plains. A few years later, her son Jonathan discovered *Homo habilis* ("able man") at the same sedimentary level of Olduvai. In comparison with *Zinjanthropus*, *Homo habilis* was a highly skilled toolmaker. Both creatures lived at various eastern African locations during

Figure 1.1. The Great Rift Valley.

the Lower Pleistocene epoch, between 3 million and 1 million years ago, and the latter is thought to be a direct ancestor of *Homo sapiens*.

Tanzania played host to the first chapter of the human saga. Unfortunately, no lineal connection can yet be made between the ancient hominids of Olduvai and the people who later populated eastern Africa and the rest of the world. As far as we now know, the human history of Tanzania began about 10,000 years ago, when Khoisan-speaking hunters and gatherers settled sparsely along the eastern Rift to the south of Olduvai. These forerunners of the modern Hadzapi and Sandawe peoples may have been the first Tanzanians.

The Settling of Mainland Tanzania

From the beginning of the first millennium B.C., the Great Rift Valley served as a highway along which immigrants passed into the sparsely inhabited northern and western portions of what is now mainland Tanzania. The first new arrivals were a Cushitic-speaking people from southern Ethiopia, who migrated through the eastern Rift until they reached a part of north-central Tanzania that was already occupied by the Khoisan hunters and gatherers. As cattle herders, these migrants found an ecological niche in the virgin grasslands of the north and lived interspersed with their neighbors in much the same way that the modern Burungi, Iraqw, and Gorowa Cushitic-speakers today share the same space with the Khoisan Hadzapi and Sandawe.

By the first millennium A.D., a much larger influx was beginning from the west, composed of Bantu-speaking peoples who probably originated in what is now southern Nigeria and Cameroon. These were iron-working agriculturalists who preferred the wetter areas of western Tanzania and, to some extent, the fertile volcanic mountains of the northeast. The Bantu were thus spared the necessity of competing with the established hunters, gatherers, and pastoralists of the dry savanna.

This balance of people and land use was disturbed between the tenth and eighteenth centuries by a succession of Central Sudanic, Nilotic, and Paranilotic migrations from the north and northwest.[2] These peoples included both grain producers and cattle keepers, who infiltrated the western and northern parts of mainland Tanzania, competed and biologically interacted with the Bantu-speakers already living there, and gradually spread into the southern and southwestern highlands. The same process of migration, conflict, and partial assimilation occurred east of the Rift, until the northeastern highlands were populated by sedentary farming communities bordered by seminomadic groups of pastoralists. The chief survivors of these early herders are the modern Masai, who also roam over a large area in the northwest. The lowlands adjacent to the Indian Ocean coast were occupied by small societies of Bantu-speaking cultivators.

Because of the constant movement and mixing of peoples between the tenth and nineteenth centuries, it is in most cases not possible to trace the cultural origins of Tanzania's contemporary ethnic groups. One demographic consistency does emerge from the time when the mainland was first settled. The highest human population densities were established at the periphery of the country, with relatively few people inhabiting the arid steppe between the eastern and western branches of the Great Rift Valley. This historic settlement pattern bears important implications for social, economic, and political relations in modern Tanzania.

Zanzibar and the Coast

The early societies of the Tanzanian coast and offshore islands, facing eastward instead of toward Africa, evolved quite differently from those of the interior.[3] Before 500 A.D., written reference was made to what is now coastal Tanzania in the *Periplus of the Erythraean Sea*, a Greek traders' guide. It is fairly certain that still earlier visits were made by merchants from Egypt, Assyria, Phoenicia, Greece, India, Arabia, and Persia. By the ninth century, Arabs and Shirazi Persians were trading regularly with the coastal peoples; they eventually established a string of settlements on the islands of Pemba, Zanzibar, Mafia, and Kilwa Kisiwani. As these outposts became permanent settlements, the Arab and Shirazi communities intermingled with the Bantu-speaking mainland groups, and a new culture—the Swahili—began to emerge.[4] By the thirteenth century, the Shirazi-ruled city-state of Kilwa Kisiwani controlled the entire eastern African trade in gold, ivory, slaves, and other up-country products. Kilwa's dominance lasted until the fifteenth century, when the Arab city-states of Zanzibar and Mombasa (in what is now Kenya) gained ascendancy.

Portuguese conquest of the coast delayed the further development of the increasingly Africanized Arab hegemony. The explorer Vasco da Gama first visited eastern Africa in 1498, and by 1506 Portugal had taken control of the city-states and their Indian Ocean trade. Portuguese suzerainty over the Tanzanian coast was lengthy but tenuous. By 1729, a group of Omani Arabs had seized power over all settlements north of the Ruvuma River, which later became the boundary separating Tanzania from the Portuguese colony of Mozambique. Omani domination of the coast continued into the nineteenth century under the aggressive Busaidi dynasty. During this time, trade increased with the interior and began with the United States and several European countries. Recognizing the potential of this trade, Sultan Said (1791–1856; reign, 1806–1856) transferred his capital from Oman to Zanzibar in 1840. There he sponsored the development of a slave-dependent plantation economy that quickly made Zanzibar the world's leading producer of cloves. Said also extended commercial relations with the mainland, emphasizing the slave trade for the first time and enlisting the support of several particularly acquisitive African societies, including the Nyamwezi of central Tanzania. By the early 1850s an important trading center had been established at Tabora, in the heart of Nyamwezi country.

Mainland Tanzania experienced its last great migration in the 1840s, when the southern African Ngoni crossed into Rukwa and proceeded to conquer and mix with peoples living in a vast area between the southern coast and Lake Tanganyika. The invasion actually furthered Zanzibar's commercial involvements on the mainland to the extent that some Ngoni enthusiastically participated in the slave trade. Far more powerful invaders were required to destroy this blossoming mercantile empire. These were the colonizing Europeans.

THE EARLY COLONIAL PERIOD

The colonial "scramble" for Africa began in a rather desultory manner throughout the continent, and no less so in Tanzania where Europeans and Americans pursued limited interests for more than fifty years before the establishment of full-scale colonial rule. Chief among these early interests was trade, which focused outside attention on Zanzibar and the commercial network controlled by Sultan Said. On the basis of private-sector initiatives and a treaty concluded with Said in 1833, the United States opened a consulate on Zanzibar in 1837. Britain followed suit in 1841, a move that allowed her freer access to the Tanzanian trade and permitted more effective implementation of the Moresby Treaty of 1822, the Anglo-Zanzibari treaty that formalized Britain's attempt to eliminate the eastern African slave trade. Zanzibar agreed to free trade treaties with France in 1844 and the Hanseatic German republics in 1859. Trade and the political influence of the British continued to expand until formal colonial rule was established.

Using Zanzibar as a point of departure, European explorers and missionaries penetrated the mainland during the middle and late nineteenth century. If sometimes inadvertently, secular and proselytizing explorers helped to define future colonial boundaries. They also paved the way for Protestant and Roman Catholic missionaries. Although their achievements in religious conversion were lackluster, the missionaries made two important contributions to the massive socioeconomic and political changes that were about to occur. First, beginning with David Livingstone, some missionaries supplemented their spiritual messages with practical instruction in the mechanical and agricultural arts. Second, others identified a potential lingua franca in the coastal Kiswahili language, itself a mixture of Bantu, Arabic, and other tongues. Missionaries transliterated Kiswahili from Arabic script into the Roman alphabet, providing a useful tool for colonial administration and economic exploitation.

German East Africa

By the early 1880s, a newly unified Germany was searching for socioeconomic *lebensraum* and a political place in the sun vis-à-vis other European powers. These needs persuaded Chancellor Otto von Bismarck to support the entrepreneurial efforts of one Karl Peters and his Society for German Colonization. Peters proceeded to the area of mainland Tanzania in 1884 and signed a series of agreements with local rulers that ceded administrative and commercial "protection" to the society. In 1885 the society was granted a German government charter to administer a largely undefined territory on the mainland, which it transferred to a new organization formed by Peters, the German East Africa Company.

This display of German ambition gave pause to the British and even more so to the sultan, Barghash (1833–1888; reign, 1870–1888), who correctly interpreted it as a direct threat to Zanzibar's mainland trading empire. Typically, the German and British governments met without consulting the sultan and agreed to the establishment of a German protectorate north of the Ruvuma River and south of what is now the international boundary dividing Kenya and Tanzania. An Anglo-German agreement of 1886 permitted the sultan to retain control over Zanzibar, Pemba, Mafia, and Lamu islands, in addition to a coastal strip extending 6 kilometers (3.5 miles) inland. In 1888 the Germans forced the sultan to grant a fifty-year lease on the coastal strip and thereby gained full economic and political jurisdiction over the mainland.

After five years of merciless economic exploitation, political oppression, and local tax revolts in the coastal towns, the German East Africa Company found itself near insolvency and under increasing attack in the German Reichstag. In 1891 the German government reluctantly assumed administrative responsibility for German East Africa, following a further Anglo-German agreement that fixed the colony's western boundaries, instituted a British protectorate over Zanzibar, and gave Germany permanent ownership of the coastal strip. The German eagle now flew over all of mainland Tanzania as well as an area that Germany lost to Belgium after World War I and that eventually became the independent states of Rwanda and Burundi.

At first organized under military leadership, the German colonial regime quickly achieved a reputation for both political ruthlessness and developmental achievement.[5] As they sought to establish effective rule, German commanders found that many of Tanzania's African societies were not hierarchically structured and possessed few institutions of formal government. For the sake of administrative efficiency and to compensate for a lack of German personnel, a local government system was created that placed Swahili and Arab agents, the *maakida*, in direct charge of locally recruited headmen, termed *majumbe*. In places where powerful African chiefs were discovered, these were incorporated into the administration under the supervision of *maakida*.

From the point of initial contact, African resistance had been mounted against the Germans and subsequently against this system of alien rule that placed not only Europeans but also Arabs and coastal Africans into locally unfamiliar positions of almost unlimited power. At a time when German military expeditions were still trying to pacify the interior, the Hehe people of present-day Iringa Region were also expanding by conquest. An armed conflict between the Hehe and the Germans ensued; it lasted from 1891 until the Hehe were defeated in 1898. Other rebellions occurred in response to the newly organized colonial government and to the agricultural and commercial interests it was intended to serve.

The initial economic policy emphasis was on European plantation agriculture, although African cash cropping was also permitted in areas where Europeans had not yet settled. The first farms were near the coast and in the fertile and comparatively temperate northeastern highlands, between the Usambara Mountains and Kilimanjaro. Here coffee, cotton, sisal, and rubber became the favored crops. The commercialization of these enterprises and a further expansion of European farming required efficient transportation facilities and readily available land and labor. The colonial government approached the transportation problem by developing a northern road network. A railroad was also completed in 1911 from the port of Tanga to Moshi, a garrison town at the base of Kilimanjaro. Another railroad was constructed to link western Tanzania with the colonial capital at Dar es Salaam. By 1914 this line reached Kigoma on Lake Tanganyika, opening a vast territory to European settlement.

As the colony was made more accessible, the rate of German immigration increased. To provide for this growth, large tracts of arable land were confiscated—or, as the British later put it more delicately, "alienated"—from African cultivators and herders. With the assistance of the *maakida*, labor was recruited by impressment and through the less direct but no less effective means of the hut tax. Africans could work off the tax or pay it by earning the necessary money. Land confiscation and this form of indentured servitude led to considerable unrest and contributed to German East Africa's most serious uprising, the Maji Maji Rebellion of 1905. The rebellion took place south of the railroad that was being built to Kigoma. Violence began near the coast and rapidly spread up-country. By 1907, the conflict had engulfed an area that today includes most of Morogoro and Ruvuma regions. *Maji* is the Kiswahili word for water, and the revolt took its name from a commonly held belief that a medicine of water and grain could ward off European bullets. Focusing their fury on all outsiders, the rebels attacked Arabs and Swahili Africans as well as European farmers and missionaries. The Germans retaliated with a scorched earth campaign that left many thousands dead from military action, disease, and famine.

The horror of Maji Maji and its suppression caused a public outcry in Germany. It contributed to the belated creation of a colonial office in Berlin and led to the appointment of German East Africa's first civilian governor, Albrecht Freiherr von Rechenberg. This professional diplomat introduced sweeping reforms

Figure 1.2. Lake Victoria near Mwanza, Symbolizing the Kiswahili Meaning of Tanganyika—
"Sail in the Wilderness."

in the treatment of Africans and a developmental policy that emphasized African
agricultural production. Among Rechenberg's innovations were directives protecting African land tenure and prohibiting forced labor except for public works
projects. Other regulations limited the private use of corporal punishment and improved working conditions for African participants in the European sector.
Africans also benefited from an expansion of formal education; more than 6,000
students were enrolled in government schools and more than 150,000 in mission
schools by 1914.[6]

These changes were vigorously opposed by the settlers, who faced severe
reductions in available land and African labor. The settlers reacted politically,
forcing Rechenberg's resignation and in the process raising the classic colonial dilemma of whether colonies should be dominated by white immigrants or by a
white government in support of the indigenous population. For the Germans at
least, World War I rendered a choice unnecessary.

Germany's defeat in the war ended her colonial interlude in eastern Africa,
despite a brilliant guerrilla action carried out against the British and their allies by
the *askari* (African soldiers) of Major General Paul von Lettow-Vorbeck and his
handful of German officers.[7] Britain occupied most of German East Africa during
the war, renamed it Tanganyika in 1920, and began constructing an administrative organization that was legitimated in 1922 when the League of Nations con-
signed Tanganyika to the British Empire. Tanganyika was not a colony in the for-

mal sense but an internationally mandated territory to be administered in the interests of "peace, order and good government" and of "the material and moral well-being and the social progress of its inhabitants."[8] For all practical purposes, however, Britain had gained another colony and now governed all of modern Tanzania.

Zanzibar Protectorate

While the Germans were occupied on the mainland, the British were making their own mark on Zanzibar. Under the terms of the 1890 protectorate agreement, Britain was supposed to manage only Zanzibari foreign affairs. Domestic relations and succession to the sultanate were left to the sultan's government. The British never took this division of responsibilities seriously, and in 1896 they installed an unabashed anglophile, Hamoud bin Muhammed (1851–1902; reign, 1896–1902), as sultan. Having devised ways legally to abolish slavery without seriously disrupting the local social and economic systems, the protectorate government induced Hamoud to sign an antislavery decree in 1897. Zanzibar's de facto colonial status was confirmed in 1913, when responsibility for the protectorate was transferred from the British Foreign Office to the Colonial Office and a resident was appointed to replace the consul general.

Although the islands were thus placed firmly under colonial control, they continued to be regarded as Arab enclaves, not as part of colonial Africa. The sultan was retained as titular head of state, and Arabs were offered the best educational opportunities and favored access to government jobs. The clove economy remained in Arab hands, and various degrees of involuntary servitude were still tolerated to provide labor for the plantations. Zanzibar's special status created a duality in Britain's eastern African imperial policy, which was reinforced as Britain assumed jurisdiction over the Tanzanian mainland. Treating Zanzibar as an Arab state also perpetuated racial and ethnic inequalities that would later bring civil strife to the islands and complicate the postindependence unification of Zanzibar with Tanganyika.

THE MAINLAND UNDER MANDATE

After the war, the densely settled western kingdoms of Ruanda and Urundi were mandated to Belgium by the League of Nations. Britain was made responsible for a mainland area of 942,618 square kilometers (377,047 square miles) and an African population that in 1921 was estimated at 4,107,000. Tanganyika's total population was rounded out by an additional 2,447 Europeans and by 14,991 Indians, Arabs, and other Asians who had originally settled in eastern Africa as traders and colonial laborers.[9] World War I had upset socioeconomic and political relations within and among these racial communities, and it was not until the mid-1920s that systematic government was restored to the mainland.

Colonial Administration Through Indirect Rule

Sir Donald Cameron was appointed governor of Tanganyika Territory in 1925 and proceeded immediately to introduce a form of local administration that he had helped develop during his earlier service in Nigeria. Cameron termed this system "indirect administration" (more commonly known as "indirect rule"). He outlined its purposes in these words:

> The Mandatory Power is under a solemn obligation so to train the natives that they may stand by themselves . . . and it seems obvious that in doing the latter, the wise course, if not the only practical course, is to build on the institutions of the people themselves, tribal institutions which have been handed down to them through the centuries. If we set up artificial institutions, these institutions can have no inherent stability and must crumble away at the first shock which they may receive. It is our duty to do everything in our power to develop the native politically on lines suitable to the state of society in which he lives.[10]

These intentions were not as static as they seem. Cameron and his successors looked to a future when traditional political institutions would evolve into democratically elected instruments of social and economic development. But two inherent shortcomings prevented indirect rule from providing the basis for democratic and developmentally oriented local government units.

In the first place, the ordinance that gave legal form to Cameron's concept authorized several types of "native authority." Each type was composed of one or more African officials who were supposed to implement colonial directives, together with whatever customary laws were not officially prohibited. All native authorities were empowered to make local bylaws and to establish courts and treasuries. Some were assisted in their duties by African advisory councils appointed by colonial administrators.[11]

As the primary goal was to recruit traditionally legitimate authority figures, the job at hand was to identify these people and install them in public office. Administrative efficiency required the appointment of one or only a few such leaders in any given locality. Chiefs, therefore, were favored over the councils of elders that governed many African communities and over clan heads who also proliferated but whose power was too limited to make them effective colonial agents. The problem was that traditional chiefs were not easy to locate. Formal political systems had never evolved in many local societies. In others migration, war, the slave trade, and German pacification policies had disrupted organized political authority. Where no genuine chiefs were found, the government appointed its own choices in the hope that they would come to be considered legitimate. The spirit of indirect rule was sacrificed to this expedient, the new elites being as foreign to the people as were the *maakida* and *majumbe* who preceded them. To worsen matters, some native authorities freely engaged in the economic exploitation of their subjects, with the passive and sometimes active complicity of the government.

The second practical difficulty with indirect rule was that both traditional and nontraditional rulers found it difficult to understand and value colonial policy and to accommodate European directives without compromising their local acceptability.[12] The native authorities were left with only two alternatives: to promote their own and the government's interests or to resist official policy when it conflicted with the customs and goals of their constituents. Unless it was done with consummate political skill, pursuing either of these options frequently resulted in administrative failure and removal from office.

For most Africans, indirect rule tightly restricted the scope and direction of political change in an otherwise rapidly changing society. Only by moving outside the immediate political context could some Tanganyikans begin the long journey toward social, economic, and political modernization.

Socioeconomic Change in the Interwar Years

By the early 1930s, a racially stratified economic system had emerged: Europeans and Asians controlled the productive and retail trade sectors and Africans increasingly participated in small-scale commercial agriculture. Like the Germans before them, British agricultural officers encouraged coffee production by the Chagga people of Kilimanjaro and the Haya on the western shore of Lake Victoria. Food crops were not emphasized anywhere because of the priority given increased agricultural revenues in imperial policy. For the same reason, and because of the relatively high population densities in African cash-crop areas, educational and other social services tended also to be concentrated among cash-crop producers.

African cooperative societies were established under official supervision to facilitate the production and marketing of export crops. These institutions acquainted their members with the functioning of modern secondary associations, and this experience proved useful as organizational horizons were expanded to include special-interest groups. Although educational opportunities were curtailed during the depression of the 1930s, a growing number of comparatively well-educated rural dwellers were attracted to Tanganyika's administrative and trading centers and there sought employment as laborers, teachers, and minor civil servants. An urbanizing subculture emerged, whose members quickly began to search for new associational forms to articulate their social and economic concerns.

The Beginnings of Political Protest

The initial colonial attitude toward African voluntary associations was expressed in an official policy statement by one of Cameron's immediate successors.

> These African Associations crop up regularly from time to time, generally under the auspices of semi-literate politically-minded mission-trained youths. . . . It is important to see that they are handled properly, i.e., with a due amount of sympathy and support for what is legitimate and prompted by reasonable motives and a due amount of firmness for what is not. They are inevitable and the best line is to deflect their energies and aspirations of their members into the paths of social welfare and away from politics and supererogation.[13]

This rather heavy-handed paternalism suggests that the British were not very worried about African interest groups. Although they were at first composed of the more educated members of single indigenous societies, the associations were not tribal groups. Rather, they were formed to help satisfy the social and material needs of increasingly marginalized men and women, who shared aspirations in the colonial economy and occupational structure but were frustrated by a lack of opportunity in the new order and by traditional social restrictions at home.

One such organization was the Bukoba Bahaya Union, formed in 1924 by a few formally educated Haya residents of Bukoba District in what is now West Lake Region. The union's stated goals were "the development of our country and . . . the seeking of a system for the simple way to civilization to our mutual advantage."[14] Members lobbied for higher coffee prices, lower taxes, freer access to land, and more urban job opportunities. They also regularly found themselves opposed to both the native and British authorities of Bukoba District.

The Bahaya Union was the most active monoethnic association to arise before 1945. An ethnically diverse group, the Tanganyika African Association (TAA), came into existence between 1927 and 1929 in the cities of Tanga and Dar es Salaam. The TAA began as a private welfare agency and social club for minor civil servants and coastal urban workers. The colonial government endorsed its modest purposes, and in the 1930s TAA branches were opened in the up-country towns of Dodoma, Kondoa, Singida, and Mpwapwa. In 1939, the association affiliated itself with the Zanzibari African Association and entered into a loose alliance with the Bahaya Union; the government began to suspect that the TAA might not forever limit its activities to urban welfare and recreation. The TAA did not become politically active until after World War II. It then expanded its membership to include rural Africans and formed the nucleus of an overtly anticolonial political party that would finally bring national independence to the mainland—the Tanganyika African National Union.

ZANZIBAR BETWEEN THE WARS

In comparison with that on the mainland, socioeconomic and political change proceeded at a snail's pace on Zanzibar.[15] The British continued to treat the islands as an Arab state, and a rigidly stratified public service was institutionalized in which Europeans held the highest posts, Arabs occupied the senior and middle-level positions, and Indians filled the lesser roles. Nearly 80 percent of the total population were Africans, who were differentiated into two groups, native Zanzibaris and recent migrants from the mainland. A racially mixed Shirazi community led the former group, which identified closely with Islam and the sultan and enjoyed a higher social status than the mainlanders. Nevertheless, the Shirazis were themselves almost totally excluded from nonmenial participation in Zanzibar's public and private sectors. Arabs maintained control over the plantation economy, and Indian traders dominated the protectorate's commercial affairs. Indians also provided credit to Arab planters, and by the late 1930s they owned mortgages on many Arab holdings.

When voluntary associations appeared, they were based on existing racial and ethnic cleavages. The Indian Association was formed in 1910 to promote its members' commercial and financial interests. The Arab Association was organized in the 1920s, at first to seek compensation from the British for economic losses suffered during the partial abolition of slavery. During the depression of the 1930s, the association sought to defend Arab land interests against the claims of Indian creditors. Reflecting its internal divisions, the African population produced two organizations. The Zanzibari African Association was founded in 1934 by mainland migrants, and the Shirazis created their own association in 1939. Both were private welfare organizations and did not develop political goals until after World War II. The African Association maintained close ties with the urban African communities of the mainland, presaging the future unification of Tanganyika and Zanzibar when it affiliated with the Tanganyika African Association in 1939.

In spite of these associational innovations, Zanzibar remained essentially as it had been for the African majority—a British colonial outpost superimposed upon and protecting a local Arab dictatorship. This arrangement became increasingly anachronistic after World War II, when it was successfully challenged and its remnants destroyed in a violent Afro-Arab revolution.

POSTWAR TANGANYIKA

Immediately following World War II, the Colonial Office set two policy requirements for Tanganyika. First, the mainland would have to supply increased quantities of agricultural products to Britain, whose economy had been weakened by the war. The second imperative related to Tanganyika's change in legal status from a mandated territory under the now defunct League of Nations to a trust territory of the newly formed United Nations Organization. Under this new arrangement, Tanganyika would soon be expected to show progress toward internal self-government and eventual independence.

The government in Dar es Salaam concluded that simultaneous action on both requirements would necessitate unprecedented levels of cooperation on the part of all Tanganyikans, regardless of race and socioeconomic position. It also became clear that Tanganyika's racially biased economy and essentially unrepresentative and unpopular native authorities could not serve either requirement and might even endanger future British influence over the mainland. In response, the government established three modest policies that set the tone for the final fifteen years of colonial rule. These policies involved accelerated agricultural and rural development, representative local government, and "multiracialism."

Agricultural and Rural Development

A ten-year development plan was introduced in 1946, which for the first time stressed primary and secondary education to prepare the African community for greater involvement in the cash economy. The colonial administration also experimented with large-scale food-oil production during the late 1940s and early 1950s and flirted with the idea of additional European settlement on the Sanya Plains between Kilimanjaro and Mt. Meru. The first scheme failed for a variety of technical and economic reasons. The second was quietly shelved after unexpectedly vocal protest by the Meru people, whose land was being confiscated to provide space for European farms.[16] The government continued to encourage European agribusiness in the privately capitalized sisal industry, but in 1955 it published a development plan that finally promised increased funding for African agriculture. In 1960, a four-year plan was devised to extend this commitment according to an agricultural "improvement approach" recently recommended by the World Bank.[17]

Neither of these plans was a detailed blueprint for economic and social change. Like earlier statements, each was a broad declaration of intent to be particularized and budgeted on a project-by-project basis. Both documents departed from previous efforts in two important respects: They focused attention on increases in African productivity, and they rejected compulsion in favor of persuasion and incentive as the primary means of achieving compliance. A former agricultural officer later reflected on the wisdom of this shift in approach.

> One basic difficulty about agricultural improvement by legislation is that it makes the Agricultural Officers unpopular and becomes a platform for opposition. . . . In the last few years, however, there has been a steady improvement in the relationship between the agricultural field staff and the farmer. The policy has been to get away from being policemen to being teachers and advisors of the farmer.[18]

This rethinking of the colonial relationship was not accompanied by an apreciable increase in developmental expenditures, and tensions grew in rural Tanganyika. African cooperative societies multiplied during the 1950s, encouraged by the Social Development Department's instruction that "the people should carry out their own betterment schemes, led by their own leaders, mobilizing their own resources, and drawing on the assistance available to them from local and central Government."[19] Yet this assistance lagged behind, and agricultural prices remained low. Intensified cultivation under traditional land-use methods resulted in soil depletion and erosion, and existing systems of land transfer fragmented farm holdings into hopelessly uneconomic plots. The native authorities were ordered to control both problems by enforcing unpopular conservation and land-tenure regulations and in the process incited local opposition that sometimes became violent.[20]

As its name implies, the improvement approach was never intended to transform the agrarian economy of Tanganyika, and the socioeconomic dislocations of uneven and incomplete modernization were not well considered in a policy that sought to achieve only the "foundations for future growth of output and income rather than immediate increases in either."[21] These dislocations help to explain why an urban-based independence movement swept so quickly through the rural areas during the late 1950s.

Local Government Reform

Not surprisingly in view of the new obligations placed upon Tanganyika's meager administrative and financial resources, the postwar policy process was heavily centralized in Dar es Salaam and the provincial capitals. As a result, district and native authorities found themselves less and less able to adapt goals of colonial policy to fit local conditions. The importance of this centralizing trend was not lost on the emerging subculture of educated Africans, who were developing new aspirations. They recognized the territorial political arena as the only real platform from which to express their dissatisfaction with the barriers erected in support of colonial rule. An informal but effective color bar prevented Africans from rising in the public service. The economic sector was blocked by an Asian entrepreneurial elite, which was encouraged by the colonial authorities partly to provide a socioeconomic buffer between them and the African community. Finally, the local political level was still dominated by conservative native authorities who reacted unsympathetically to demands for change.

The government strongly discouraged African participation in territorial politics. The official intent was for political modernization to evolve through efficient and democratically elected local government bodies. Toward this end, partly elected councils were instituted during the early 1950s in an attempt to prepare for future reforms within the temporarily stabilizing context of the native authority system. Few of these councils were taken seriously enough to justify their continuance or to retard the growth of a progressively more unified African opposition movement. Instead, they symbolized an increasingly obvious contradiction in official attitudes toward socioeconomic and political change. On the one hand, political participation was acknowledged as an inevitable consequence of expanded formal education, involvement in the cash economy, and physical mobility. On the other hand, the two greatest obstacles to effective participation had to be preserved in the interests of stability and the very survival of the regime. These were the government chiefs and a racially differentiated society. Time began to run out for both the native authorities and Britain's genteel racism when the Tanganyika African National Union (TANU) appeared on the scene.

Nationalism, "Multiracialism," and Independence

From the outset an anticolonial movement, TANU evolved from a proliferation of protopolitical interest groups. By 1952, ethnic associations similar to the Bukoba Bahaya Union had been formed by the Chagga, Sukuma, Sambaa, Meru, and Zaramo peoples. The multiethnic Tanganyika African Association, which had assimilated several rural ethnic organizations during the late 1940s, had expanded its purview to include such compelling political problems as the possibility of increased white settlement in postwar Tanganyika and recent efforts by Kenyan and Tanganyikan whites to join the two territories under one government. The TAA took additional stands favoring the abolition of compulsory labor on public works projects and criticizing the inadequacy of agricultural and rural educational programs for Africans. This is not to imply that the TAA was developing into a well-integrated territorial movement. The Mashomvi and Mashah branches, for example, refused to cooperate with the Zaramo branch following a disagreement over which would represent the coastal area in dealings with the government, and the Zanzibar branch claimed that it was the TAA's "parent body" and then seceded from the mainland organization.

The TAA achieved only limited success in attracting its communally organized branches into one cohesive union. Nevertheless, by the early 1950s these factions had become accustomed to opposing government policy when it conflicted with the immediate concerns of their members. Responding to an anxious British inquiry, the TAA underscored the growing importance of this approach. "It is becoming more necessary these days for Africans to organize themselves into bodies to formulate their opinions on the major issues vitally affecting their interests."[22] Branches in Arusha, Bukoba, Upare, Sukumaland, and elsewhere protested regulations limiting crop and livestock production and campaigned against the native authorities. In Sukumaland, cooperative societies joined with the TAA in the same kinds of protest. Against this background TANU was formed in July 1954 on what later became celebrated as Saba Saba Day—the seventh day of the seventh month.

For its part, the colonial government still clung to the idea of limiting African political participation to the local level. "It is Government's policy to develop responsible local government at all levels, so that as many people as possible may learn how to manage for themselves the affairs of their areas. In the Legislative Council at Dar es Salaam constitutional changes will continue to be introduced when the time is ripe and these changes will lead in the first place to representative local government."[23] Under these rather unrealistic guidelines, provincial commissioners were expected to curtail local opposition and at the same time reverse the unifying trend in African interest politics. The new TANU elites sought further unification on the basis of nonethnic party loyalty and began a full-scale political campaign against the colonial regime. The administration replied by closing party branches in ten districts under a vaguely worded amendment to the penal code banning publications and statements "likely to raise discontent among any of the inhabitants of the territory."[24] This harassment proved fruitless as interest groups and TAA branches rushed to affiliate with TANU. By 1958 the party claimed 134 branches scattered throughout Tanganyika.

TANU's organizational growth is made even more remarkable by the early shortage of party leadership. In another attempt to slow the spread of nationalism, the government prohibited public servants from joining political organizations. This restriction separated TANU from a large pool of potential organizers and forced it to operate with only a handful of former TAA and other stalwarts who either were not government employees or were prepared to sacrifice their jobs. TANU president Julius K. Nyerere was obliged to make the latter choice.

As the son of a government chief, Nyerere had been afforded special educational opportunities at the Tabora Government School. He went on to Makerere College and from there to Edinburgh University, where he earned two social science degrees between 1949 and 1952. Nyerere returned to Tanganyika in 1952 and became president of the TAA in 1953. At his initiative, the TAA was absorbed in July 1954 into the new TANU organization. Nyerere had become a teacher at St. Francis College, Pugu, a Roman Catholic secondary school near Dar es Salaam. Because of his political activities, strong official pressure was exerted on the mission authorities for his dismissal. Nyerere resigned from his teaching position in 1955 to become a full-time politician. He was joined by a small number of well-educated and highly energetic colleagues, whose seemingly endless travels and speeches thoroughly overwhelmed British attempts to stop the TANU bandwagon.

TANU's organizational successes were not matched by its ability to control its local branches. Opposition to colonial policy was producing its own multiplier effect during the middle 1950s, and the TANU leadership was no less surprised than the government by the eagerness of physically isolated communities to identify with it. TANU was also intended to be a mass movement, not a doctrinally specific vanguard party. Of necessity and to some extent by design, each branch enjoyed considerable autonomy, which sometimes made it difficult to coordinate strategies and tactics devised in Dar es Salaam. TANU commanded massive if sometimes unwieldy support in the independence confrontation, and with this backing it was able to hasten Britain's departure from Tanganyika. The problem of local political separatism was to endure after independence.

TANU's immediate goal was to attain self-government on the basis of a majoritarian principle that ignored the ethnic and racial divisions employed by the British to perpetuate colonial rule. Under continuing UN scrutiny and with TANU making direct appeals to the Trusteeship Council and the General Assembly, Britain recognized the inevitability of self-government. The British, however, had already adopted a "multiracial" policy line, similar to what they were attempting in other eastern and central African colonies with much larger European populations. The Tanganyikan version of multiracialism was the brainchild of Governor Sir Edward Twining. He took office in 1949 and immediately set about requiring racial parity on all local councils, despite the absence of Asians and Europeans in many districts. Constitutional development through the equal representation of demographically unequal racial groups furnished a ready target for TANU, which adopted as one of its major objectives the achievement of African majorities on all elective local government bodies. Multiracialism also gave Julius Nyerere a concrete issue to present before the United Nations. Here he received support for the position that this policy was not in keeping with the conception of self-government envisioned in the trusteeship agreement.

By 1955, the United Nations and the Colonial Office had both requested that elections be held for the selection of unofficial delegates to the Tanganyika Legislative Council, a territorial advisory body dominated by non-African government officers, farmers, and businessmen. Anticipating these elections, Governor Twining encouraged a group of Europeans and Asians to form the United Tanganyika party (UTP) in order to provide TANU with organized electoral competition. In an attempt to enlist UTP support from the loyalist African community, Twining declared that the prohibition on political participation by public servants did not include native authority chiefs.

Under a franchise tightly restricted according to income and education, only 60,000 voters were registered to participate in the election, which was held in two phases during 1958 and 1959. TANU at first decided not to contest an election that reserved ten of the available thirty seats for Europeans and ten for Asians, but it ultimately campaigned not only for its own candidates but also for Europeans and Asians who opposed UTP. The government continued to intimidate TANU during the campaign and even convicted Nyerere of libel when he criticized two British district commissioners in the TANU newsletter. The mounting political tensions were relieved when Governor Twining was replaced by Sir Richard Turnbull, a moderate with instructions expeditiously to prepare Tanganyika for self-rule. Turnbull's first task was to preside over an election in which African voters outnumbered non-Africans, in spite of the high registration requirements. When the votes were tallied, TANU or TANU-supported candidates were returned to all thirty of the elected Legislative Council seats. Turnbull announced that racial parity was unnecessary on local councils and that territorial-level multiracialism was but a temporary measure to secure an orderly transfer to nonracial majority rule. In the meantime, UTP had quietly disbanded.

A new franchise was announced in 1959, and another election was set for August 1960. This time nearly 1 million people qualified to vote for an elected majority of the Legislative Council. Fifty of the seventy-one elected seats could be contested by candidates of any race, eleven were reserved for Asian candidates, and ten for Europeans. A prototype cabinet of ten unofficial ministers was to be chosen from the elected majority. They would be joined by an official delegation consisting of the deputy govenor and two other senior colonial officers. TANU candidates ran unopposed in fifty-eight of the seventy-one contests and lost only one of the remaining thirteen races. Nyerere was appointed chief minister, and under his leadership swift progress was made toward independence. Internal self-government was proclaimed on May 15, 1961; Nyerere was appointed prime minister and placed in charge of domestic affairs. The colonial government retained control over foreign relations and the military until December 9, when Tanganyika became fully independent.

TOWARD INDEPENDENCE AND REVOLUTION ON ZANZIBAR

In comparison with Zanzibar's advance to independence, Tanganyika's was a model of political unity. In an atmosphere of almost complete socioeconomic inertia, postwar Zanzibari politics consisted of recurrent ethnic and racial confrontations involving the British and shifting coalitions of increasingly well-organized Arabs, Shirazis, and Africans. At one point the process was stopped and Zanzibar was granted its political independence. As might be expected, this act did not result in a viable national government; it took a brief but violent revolution to establish who would rule in the name of the majority.

Communal Conflict and Party Competition

As noted earlier, the colonial government considered Zanzibar an Arab state whose integrity was protected by the British presence. Under the watchful eye of a sympathetic administration, Arabs maintained their hegemony into the postwar period. Colonial political and administrative institutions reflected this bias. From its founding in 1926, the Zanzibari Legislative Council had included an unofficial minority of members appointed largely from the Arab community, and the civil service continued to consist mostly of Arabs. The British were therefore nonplussed when the previously supportive Arab Association in 1954 published strongly anticolonial articles in its newsletter. When all but one of its executives were subsequently convicted of sedition, the association organized an eighteen-month boycott of the Legislative Council. A stated goal of the boycott was to push the British toward granting internal self-government under majority rule.

Events on the mainland may have precipitated this attempt to hasten the arrival of independence while an Arab-led coalition could still maintain control over the African majority, which was becoming increasingly politicized. Whatever factors were involved, the Arab Association launched Zanzibar into a decade of extraordinary political turmoil that quickly engulfed all ethnic groups.

The Arab Association's monopoly over oppositional politics did not last long. In 1956, a few Arab intellectuals converted a rural protest organization into the Zanzibar Nationalist Party (ZNP). The most radical faction of ZNP was led by a young Marxist, Abdul Rahman Mohammed, who was popularly if somewhat misleadingly known as Babu ("grandfather"). The Zanzibari African Association and the Shirazi Association joined in 1957 to form the Afro-Shirazi Union (ASU). Its leader was Abeid Karume, former president of the Zanzibari African Association and a native Zanzibari dockworker and labor organizer. Trade unions were themselves becoming politically more active during the 1950s; the ZNP and ASU both vied for their support.

The British sought to channel this burst of political activism into electoral competition and thus provide for an orderly transition to independence under a popular government representing, it was hoped, the sultan. The administration expanded the unofficial minority on the Legislative Council by adding six elected positions to the existing twelve appointed seats. An election was conducted in 1957, and five of the six contests were won by Africans. The ZNP won no seats and the ASU took only three. The remaining positions were filled by independents who had the backing of nonparty ethnic associations.

These inconclusive results revealed deep primordial divisions in Zanzibari politics, which ensured that "the common denominator of electoral success in any constituency was affiliation with or sponsorship by an established communal organization"[25] and not just a coalitional political party. Following the 1957 election, factional and ethnic cleavages developed within the ZNP. Similarly, the ASU was unable to hold together its confederation of Shirazis representing the islands of Pemba and Zanzibar. In 1959, the Pemba Shirazis withdrew and formed the Zanzibar and Pemba People's Party (ZPPP). Those remaining in the ASU rallied to Abeid Karume and renamed themselves the Afro-Shirazi Party (ASP).

The British responded to this confusion by again enlarging the Legislative Council, this time to create an unofficial majority of elected seats. An election was scheduled for January 1961, in which the ASP won more than 40 percent of the popular vote and ten of the twenty-two elected seats. The ZNP secured nine seats with 36 percent of the vote, and the ZPPP gained three seats with an electoral share of 17 percent. The ZPPP was thus placed in a position to determine a governing coalition, but failed when two of its elected members allied with the ZNP and one with the ASP. An exasperated colonial government added one more elected seat and set another election for June.

This time the ZPPP and ZNP campaigned together against the ASP. The battle lines were thus drawn between groups representing Arabs and Shirazis on the one hand and a much larger number of Zanzibari and mainland Africans on the other. Violence erupted when the ZNP-ZPPP coalition gained a slim majority of three seats. Sixty-eight Arabs were killed in a week of rioting. The majority coalition almost immediately began to break down on ideological grounds. Babu had recently emerged from a fifteen-month jail sentence for sabotage. Unwilling to join the ZNP in support of the sultan, he formed his own Umma (Masses) party, based on the radical Federation of Progressive Trade Unions, which he had also organized. The ASP leadership sensed future electoral victory and intensified its efforts to find support in the African community.

Evidently determining that now was as good a time as ever, the British arranged for Zanzibar to receive internal self-government in June 1963, increased the size of the Legislative Council to thirty-one elected seats, and held a final preindependence election in July. Having just been organized, Umma fielded no candidates. The ASP won more than 54 percent of the popular vote and thirteen seats, but the ZNP-ZPPP alliance received eighteen seats and was invited to form a government. Its victory was partly due to gerrymandering in the Stone Town section of Zanzibar town. Upon taking office, the new government reaffirmed its dedication to the sultanate and prepared to ban postindependence political opposition. Independence was granted on December 10, 1963.

The Zanzibari Revolution and Union with Tanganyika

The new government lasted barely a month. On January 12, 1964, a violent revolution ousted the ZNP-ZPPP regime and drove the sultan into exile in Britain. Undetermined numbers of Arabs were slain, and thousands of others were arrested and their property confiscated. Although the revolution itself was not unexpected, its leadership emerged from an unlikely source. Weakened by internal dissent, ASP failed to take a unified stand against the independence government. With the help of an ideologically more cohesive Umma elite, Babu was able to gain the loyalty of urban workers, landless peasants, and most important, a large number of Tanganyikan police officers whom the British had imported in anticipation of a postindependence insurrection. Curiously, the actual fighting was led by a Kenyan soldier of fortune, John Okello, who disappeared from the scene soon after the sultanate was overthrown and a revolutionary government established. Babu and his victorious Umma group entered into a governing alliance with a large ASP faction led by Abeid Karume. A Revolutionary Council was created, and Karume was appointed president of the People's Republic of Zanzibar and Pemba.

The international clove trade was depressed in 1964, and the Zanzibari economy was further disrupted by the revolution. Under these inauspicious circumstances, the ASP-Umma coalition sought to complete the revolution by eliminating all vestiges of racial and ethnic stratification on the islands. The plantations' productivity depended partly on such inequalities, and additional economic reversals resulted from this attempt instantly to transform Zanzibar into a classless society.

A political problem also developed as the Revolutionary Council first met. The ideologically rigid Umma socialists entered into an informal partnership with a small number of ASP militants and began to overrule the ASP leadership on domestic and foreign policy issues. President Karume appealed to Julius Nyerere; and in a power play of great portent, Karume and Nyerere met in April 1964 and concluded a constitutional agreement to unite the mainland with the islands. The new state was first called the United Republic of Tanganyika and Zanzibar; later that year it was renamed the United Republic of Tanzania. Nyerere became president of the United Republic and Karume was made one of its two vice-presidents.

The union was administratively tentative and politically shaky. Zanzibar resisted incorporation as just another Tanzanian region and to this day maintains considerable, if declining, autonomy. Still, April 1964 marks the point at which political boundaries again reflected the ties that in past centuries had joined Tanganyika and Zanzibar. With the ratification of the articles of union, the islands and the mainland became a single nation.

2

The Ecology of Change

FREEDOM AND POVERTY

To leaders and citizens alike, the independence and constitutional unification of Tanzania represented momentous but incomplete achievements. It remained for Tanzania's austere physical and economic environments to be transformed by an ethnically mixed, geographically dispersed, and rapidly growing population, which possessed few of the necessary tools to match aspirations with accomplishments.

As in the past, those who sought modernization realized that their private resources and institutions were inadequate to the task and that they would have to be supplemented by considerable assistance from the public sector. Fortunately, independence had brought significant improvements in the locus and nature of political authority. An alien and unrepresentative government had been replaced by an indigenous system whose elites were well aware of their dependence on continued popular support. As Amir Jamal, minister of state in the president's office, wrote:

> The relationship between the leaders and the masses requires to be recast fundamentally so that the dialogue between them becomes continuous as well as politically and economically productive. Once the sanctions . . . in support of colonial rule are withdrawn, a government can only govern . . . if it . . . undertakes immediately the critical task of building up an almost monolithic dialogue with the masses.[1]

Even as the political leadership acknowledged that the country's poverty was inherent and not just a distributive result of colonial exploitation, it also recognized that leadership's dialogue with the masses could not consist of mere rhetoric. If policy initiatives were to produce economic and social benefits and thereby reinforce the legitimacy of the regime, ways would have to be found of

> bridging the gap on a day-to-day basis, not between technology and subsistence economy but between those leaders who become compulsively aware of their total dependence on technology, which would take some generations' efforts to become home-based, and the masses who inevitably simplify brutally by asking in constant refrain—why can't we have the hospitals, the schools, the roads and the tractors today![2]

Unlike many other poor countries, Tanzania has never flinched from facing the most basic and persistent question of independence: Under what conditions and with what success can society be inspired to participate in the hard work of modernization, with few immediate rewards to serve as incentives and under ecological conditions that are among the world's most challenging? The political and economic responses to this question are discussed in Chapters 3 through 6. This chapter will highlight some of the environmental and social factors that have critically influenced political and economic choices.

THE PHYSICAL AND SOCIAL MILIEU

With more than 90 percent of the population living at least partly off the land, subsistence agriculture is vital to Tanzanian society. Unfortunately, much of the land will sustain none but the hardiest of food crops. The areas that are fertile support the majority of people but are becoming overcrowded to the point that food production is being endangered. Substantial increases in agricultural productivity are possible only through the application of expensive—hence scarce—developmental inputs. But the population is growing at one of the fastest rates in the world, and an increasing share of this growth is being absorbed within marginally productive urban areas that draw food and other resources from the countryside. This widening ecological imbalance has been with Tanzania since before independence and has created political and economic problems that are better appreciated through a closer look at the land and its people.

The Land

Water, soils, and insect pests limit arability in most of Tanzania. Except in the highlands, rain is usually either excessively abundant or insufficient. Even in normal years, only one-third of the mainland enjoys a 95 percent or greater probability of receiving at least 750 millimeters (30 inches) of annual rainfall, an amount considered minimal for consistently productive agriculture. At the same time, heavy rainfalls and flash flooding are common throughout much of the country. Two-thirds of Tanzania is typically too dry or too wet to permit high food-crop yields.

In addition to the problem of rainfall, many Tanzanian soils are infertile and others remain unavailable for ready use. The coastal area and islands are predominantly coralline and sandy, and soils of the eastern and central plateaus contain even fewer nutrients than the coralline and sandy soils. The more fertile valleys contain heavy and moist loams that require extensive drainage and mechanical cultivation for effective cropping. Alluvial varieties found near riverbeds also require reclamation, together with irrigation and desalinization.

Nearly 90 percent of the mainland is covered by a grass, bush, and tree savanna that is difficult and expensive to clear. More than half the country is also infested with the tsetse fly, a carrier of human and animal sleeping sickness. The fly lives in bush vegetation and hinders livestock production in areas that could otherwise support cattle, if not food plants. Selective bush clearing has been

Figure 2.1. Villagers Discussing Erosion Control. (Courtesy Tanzanian Ministry of Agriculture)

employed in the past to control tsetse, but this technique is costly and has not been widely practiced for more than a decade.

Only about 35 percent of Tanzania is well suited to food- and cash-crop production with low-input subsistence methods. This proportion is unlikely to increase significantly in the near future because of environmental constraints underscored by Ruthenberg in the mid-1960s.[3] In most areas soil fertility is insufficient to permit continuous cultivation, and bush vegetation quickly returns during the fallow periods. Less rainfall would facilitate farming and ranching by reducing unwanted bush and the tsetse fly population. Yet under present technology, more rainfall is necessary for increased crop production. The most arable and easily cultivated land lies in parts of Zanzibar, in a few locations near Lake Victoria, and in the volcanic northeastern and southern highlands. These areas have also experienced the greatest human population pressures.

Recent Demographic Trends

Tanzania has undergone four national censuses, all conducted since World War II. The census year totals depicted in Table 2.1 reveal a trend of steadily increasing population and population growth rates. Current data are not available for fertility and mortality; but at an estimated population growth rate of between 3.3 and 3.8 percent, the crude birthrate should be within a range of 50 to 54 per

THE ECOLOGY OF CHANGE

TABLE 2.1

Tanzanian Population Growth, 1948-1978

Census Year	Total Population	Annual Average Increase	Annual Average Growth Rate (%)
1948[a]	7,981,120	-	-
1957[a]	9,600,852	179,970	2.25
1967	12,313,469	271,262	2.82
1978	17,527,564	474,009	3.85[b]

Sources: Tanzania, Statistical Abstract, 1965 (Dar es Salaam: Central Statistical Bureau, Ministry of Economic Affairs and Development Planning, 1967), p. 10; and Tanzania, 1978 Population Census Preliminary Report (Dar es Salaam: Bureau of Statistics, Ministry of Finance and Planning, n.d.), p. 177.

[a]Not including Zanzibar and Pemba.

[b]According to a visiting AID population specialist, the Tanzanian director of census "believes that the crude death rate is underestimated" in this statistic, "and accepts [growth rate] figures of 3.0 to 3.3 as more probable." (Internal AID memorandum from Gary Merritt to Albert E. Henn, November 8, 1979, pp. 3-4.) The official census report reflects this cautious approach to the 1978 data, indicating an annual average growth rate of 3.3 percent between 1967 and 1978. The report adds that "due to better preparations in the 1978 census and the almost total villagization of the country, facilitating enumeration, it is the impression that the coverage in 1978 was better than in 1967. . . . Growth rates will be thoroughly analysed in a later stage of the census work." (Tanzania, 1978 Population Census Preliminary Report, op. cit., p. 34.) For the purposes of the following analysis, I have accepted the official national and regional growth rate estimates.

thousand and the crude death rate is probably 16 to 20 per thousand. Tanzanians' average life expectancy increased from 40 years in 1967 to 52 years in 1979, and their net reproduction rate grew from 2.22 in 1970 to about 2.38 in 1980.[4] As a net reproduction rate of 2.0 yields a doubled population within one generation, the Tanzanian population will reach or exceed 35 million by the year 2000.

Of particular importance for the future are the country's present age and sex distributions. In 1981, 40 percent of all Tanzanian women were in the reproductive age group of 15 to 44 years.[5] This statistic suggests that the population pressure on a relatively fixed amount of arable land will soon increase dramatically. Sex ratios vary from more than 1.0 males per 1.0 female in urban centers, which account for only about 12 percent of the total population, to less than 0.9 males per 1.0 female in the rural areas. These ratios, combined with high birth rates, declining death rates, and one of the world's highest overall growth rates, ensure that fertility will not drop to replacement level until well into the next century.[6]

Countrywide data may convey a general impression of population dynamics, but full appreciation of the differential social and economic effects of population growth requires an analysis of subnational data. Table 2.2 presents

TABLE 2.2

Tanzanian Regional Population Characteristics, 1967-1978

Region	1967 Population	1978 Population	Total Increase (%)	Annual Average Growth Rate (%)	Geographical Area in Square Kilometers	Average Density per Square Kilometer 1967	1978
Mwanza	1,055,883	1,443,418	36.7	2.9	19,683	53.6	73.3
Shinyanga	899,468	1,323,482	47.1	3.6	50,760	17.7	26.1
Mbeya	753,765	1,080,241	43.3	3.3	60,350	12.5	17.9
Tanga	771,060	1,038,592	34.7	2.7	26,677	28.9	38.9
West Lake	658,712	1,009,379	53.2	4.0	28,456	23.1	35.5
Dodoma	709,380	971,921	37.0	2.9	41,311	17.2	23.5
Morogoro	682,700	939,190	37.6	2.9	70,624	9.7	13.3
Arusha	610,474	928,478	52.1	3.9	82,098	7.4	11.3
Iringa	689,905	922,801	33.8	2.7	56,850	12.1	16.2
Kilimanjaro	652,722	902,394	38.3	3.0	13,250	49.3	68.1
Dar es Salaam	356,286	851,522	139.0	8.2	1,393	255.8	611.3
Tabora	502,068	818,049	62.9	4.5	76,150	6.6	10.7
Mtwara	621,293	771,726	24.2	2.0	16,710	37.2	46.2
Mara	544,125	723,295	32.9	2.6	21,760	25.0	33.2
Kigoma	473,443	648,950	37.1	2.9	37,040	12.8	17.5
Singida	457,938	614,030	34.1	2.7	49,340	9.3	12.4
Ruvuma	395,447	564,113	42.7	3.3	63,669	6.2	8.9
Lindi	419,853	527,902	25.7	2.1	66,040	6.4	8.0
Coast	428,041	516,949	20.8	1.7	32,547	13.2	15.9
Rukwa	276,091	451,897	63.7	4.6	68,635	4.1	6.6
Zanzibar[a]	190,494	273,365	43.5	3.3	1,660	114.8	164.7
Pemba[a]	164,321	205,870	25.3	2.1	984	167.0	209.2

Source: Tanzania, 1978 Population Census Preliminary Report (Dar es Salaam: Bureau of Statistics, Ministry of Finance and Planning, n.d.), p. 177.

[a] Combined totals for Zanzibar's three regions and Pemba's two regions.

recent demographic information on Tanzania's regions (see the map in the introduction). In 1978 as in 1967, the highest local densities were found on Zanzibar and Pemba, in the northeastern highlands near Kilimanjaro and the southern highlands near Mbeya, in the vicinity of Lake Victoria, and in the urban and hinterland areas of Tanga, Dar es Salaam, and Mtwara. An average of 5.8 people was added to each square kilometer of Tanzania between 1967 and 1978, with a range of from 355.5 in Dar es Salaam to 1.6 in Lindi. The most densely populated regions were Dar, Pemba, Zanzibar, Mwanza, Kilimanjaro, Mtwara, Tanga, and West Lake. An increasing share of the rural population resides on Tanzania's dry central and western steppes; some of the country's highest population growth rates were recorded for Rukwa, Tabora, Shinyanga, and Arusha regions.

Annual rainfall varies considerably among and within the regions, from more than 2,540 millimeters (102 inches) in parts of southern Mbeya to less than 500 millimeters (20 inches) in such areas as eastern Mwanza, western Shinyanga, Tabora, Rukwa, and Mtwara. This range is sufficient to produce nationally adequate supplies of food crops, but only if the rains are reliable. Persistent droughts and floods in recent years have again demonstrated that the rains in Tanzania are far from reliable (see Chapter 5).

In order to understand the social and economic effects of Tanzanian population growth and distribution patterns, it is necessary to supplement census data with information on the human carrying capacity of the more and less heavily settled areas. Rainfall probability is a good indicator of carrying capacity because, under conditions of a relatively unchanged subsistence technology, rainfall remains the most critical factor in food production.

Figure 2.2 indicates Tanzania's rainfall probabilities. By comparing regional population characteristics with approximations of regional rainfall probabilities, an interesting picture emerges of the regions' human ecology (see Table 2.3). In 1978, 36 percent of the population lived in the eight regions with a low average rainfall probability of 1.4. These regions account for 51 percent of Tanzania's geographical area but, in keeping with their relative aridity, had a low average population density of 17.1 people per square kilometer. With regional densities greater than the national average of 19.8 people per square kilometer, Mtwara, Shinyanga, and Dodoma were heavily populated for their rainfall probabilities. Population growth rates for the eight regions averaged 3.3 percent, the average growth rate that the government claimed for all of Tanzania. As noted earlier, however, regional populations were growing at much higher rates in Rukwa, Tabora, Shinyanga, and Arusha.

The remaining regions exhibited differing but consistent demographic and ecological patterns. High rural densities were found in comparatively dry Mwanza Region and in well-watered Pemba, Zanzibar, Kilimanjaro, and West Lake. Mwanza is especially prone to drought-related problems. This region, which is physically small, contained the greatest percentage of the national population of any region and was adding residents at an average annual rate of nearly 3 percent. In the other regions of this high-density group, rainfall is not as much of a problem as in Mwanza, but density poses an equally serious ecological hazard. Zanzibar, Pemba, Kilimanjaro, and West Lake, which include an area totaling only 5 per-

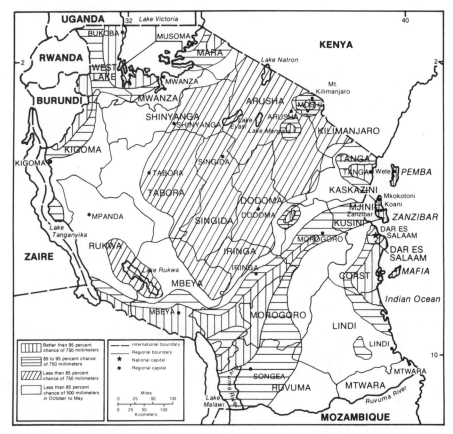

Figure 2.2. Tanzanian Annual Rainfall Probabilities.
Source: Adapted from Allison Butler Herrick et al., *Area Handbook for Tanzania* (Washington, D.C.: U.S. Government Printing Office, 1968), p. 15.

cent of the country, had populations making up 13.5 percent of the national total in 1978. With densities exceeding 100 people per square kilometer in the most arable locations, and with populations growing at an average annual rate of more than 3 percent, these parts of Tanzania were straining the carrying capacities of their moist but finite environments.

Population growth and distribution were fairly compatible with normal rainfall probabilities in the rest of Tanzania. Urban centers, with very high densities and growth rates, provided exceptions to this generalization. Unless they are environmentally accommodated, even small rural population increases will inevitably lead to permanent shortages of arable land and food and to growing dissatisfaction, political alienation, and conflict. Food-dependent urban concentrations pose their own problems of human misery and political instability. In

TABLE 2.3

Regional Population Characteristics by Regional Rainfall Probabilities, 1978

Region	Rainfall Probability Index[a]	Population (% of total)[b]	Annual Average Growth Rate (%)	Geographical Area (% of total)[b]	Average Density per Square Kilometer
Least Well-Watered					
Mtwara	1.0	4.4	2.0	1.9	46.2
Rukwa	1.0	2.6	4.6	7.7	6.6
Shinyanga	1.0	7.5	3.6	5.7	26.1
Tabora	1.0	4.7	4.5	8.6	10.7
Lindi	1.5	3.0	2.1	7.4	8.0
Marginally Well-Watered					
Dodoma	2.0	5.5	2.9	4.7	23.5
Singida	2.0	3.5	2.7	5.6	12.4
Arusha	2.0	5.3	3.9	9.3	11.3
Moderately Well-Watered					
Mwanza	2.2	8.2	2.9	2.2	73.3
Iringa	2.2	5.3	2.7	6.4	16.2
Mbeya	2.2	6.7	3.3	6.8	17.9
Tanga	2.3	5.9	2.7	3.0	38.9
Morogoro	2.3	5.3	2.9	8.0	13.3
Dar es Salaam	2.3	4.8	8.2	0.1	611.3
Mara	2.3	4.1	2.6	2.4	33.2
Kigoma	2.3	3.7	2.9	4.2	17.5
Ruvuma	2.3	3.2	3.3	7.2	8.9
Coast	2.3	2.9	1.7	3.7	15.9

			Most Well-Watered		
Kilimanjaro	3.0	5.1	3.0	1.5	68.1
West Lake	3.5	5.7	4.0	3.2	35.5
Zanzibar[c]	4.0	1.5	3.3	0.2	114.8
Pemba[c]	4.0	1.2	2.1	0.1	167.0

Source: Tanzania, 1978 Population Census Preliminary Report (Dar es Salaam: Bureau of Statistics, Ministry of Finance and Planning, n.d.), p. 177.

[a]With reference to Figure 2.1, these values represent approximations of regional rainfall probabilities during a given year. Rainfall zones with better than a 95 percent chance of receiving 750 millimeters were assigned a value of 4. Less well-watered zones were assigned values of 3, 2, and 1. Regional scores were calculated by roughly weighting each region's zonal values on a geographical basis, adding the values, and then dividing the total by the number of zones within the region. It should be emphasized that the resulting scores are only estimates, and do not take into account the unusually dry weather of recent years. However, they do accomplish their purpose of distinguishing regions with more rainfall problems from those with less.

[b]Percentages do not total 100 because of rounding.

[c]Combined totals for Zanzibar's three regions and Pemba's two regions.

1967, only 5 percent of the population lived in towns with more than 10,000 inhabitants. The average annual urban growth rate from 1948 to 1967 was 6.8 percent, compared with a total growth rate of about 2.5 percent. By 1978, the number of people living in the same towns had increased to about 12.5 percent of all Tanzanians.[7] Between 1967 and 1978 the annual urban growth rate rose to nearly 10 percent.

Not unexpectedly, Dodoma, which is intended to be the future capital, and the present capital of Dar es Salaam are among the most rapidly expanding cities. Between 1967 and 1978 the population of Dar es Salaam increased from 272,821 to 870,020 and that of Dodoma from 23,559 to 160,352. During the same period, regional capitals, such as Mbeya, Mwanza, Tanga, and Tabora, experienced similar growth.

Rapid urbanization is not caused by high urban fertility. City life may in fact reduce fertility by encouraging nuclear instead of extended families, the desire for fewer children, and unbalanced sex distributions. In 1978, thirty-one of ninety-six mainland districts contained more men than women. With two exceptions, all these districts include or are located on the outskirts of a town with more than 10,000 residents.[8] By 1967, 66 percent of all people living in such towns had been born in the rural areas.[9] Recent studies indicate that migration continues to be the major source of urban population growth and is encouraged by sizable income differences between the cities and the countryside and by large numbers of unskilled primary school leavers in search of jobs.[10] Consisting mainly of administrative hubs and entrepots, Tanzanian cities are inherently weak as generators of new wealth and employment. The plight of the urban areas is exacerbated by a marginally productive agricultural sector, which has trouble feeding even itself during lean years.

Problems of population growth and distribution will continue to strain the capacity of Tanzania's fragile and already overtaxed physical environment and in doing so create policy dilemmas that require imaginative political and economic solutions. The political and economic challenges are equally serious from the perspectives of social and cultural orientations, economic opportunities, and human settlement patterns.

The Social and Cultural Landscape

Tanzanian society is divided on a roughly equal basis among professed Christians, Muslims, and animists. Unlike large religious minorities in other countries, however, none of these groups has evolved into a self-conscious political movement. Christian missionaries favored the country's more temperate zones, where they engaged in secular education as well as religious conversion. As a result, the most educated and prosperous Tanzanians tend to be Christians.[11]

Education is highly valued in Tanzania, and the party-government hopes to achieve universal primary education by about 1985. Mass literacy campaigns have been conducted; by the mid-1970s these involved more than 3 million adults who had not previously been exposed to any formal schooling.[12] Tanzania's higher educational policies stress the development of practical skills and the combination of work with classroom study. The number of secondary school students has more than tripled since 1970, although there are places for only 10 percent of primary school graduates. Secondary curricula emphasize technical subjects, such as agriculture, home economics, and mechanics. Students qualifying for still higher educational opportunities are obliged to work for specified periods before entering each of the successively more advanced certificate, diploma, and degree programs. These too focus on the scientific and technical disciplines rather than on the liberal arts. The official intent is to satisfy the country's developmental skill requirements and at the same time prevent the growth of an educated elite class with no experience or interest in manual labor. The latter effort has proven largely successful;[13] but with room for less than 1 percent of the total population, the postsecondary educational system remains sorely inadequate to serve the pressing need for scientific, technical, and administrative leadership.

A concern with human welfare and an improved status for all age groups and both sexes is expressed in policies guaranteeing equal rights and educational opportunities and in extensive programs of general, maternal, and child health care. From well before independence, TANU insisted on equal educational access for girls and sponsored distinct suborganizations to encourage political participation among women, youth, and the elderly. These traditions have been carried over into TANU's successor party, the Chama cha Mapinduzi. Tanzanian women have always performed an essential societal role as food-crop producers. Except perhaps on Zanzibar, women are now rapidly becoming the social and economic equals of men. According to one recent law (which excludes predominantly Muslim Zanzibar), a first wife must formally register her consent before her husband can take a second wife. Unlike in the past, a wife is also legally entitled to an inheritance when her husband dies.[14]

Ethnicity is important in Tanzania, but in a somewhat different manner than in many other developing countries where mass mobilization has resulted in politically destabilizing communalism. Social mobilization and political participation are emphasized more in Tanzania than in any other African country, with the possible exception of Mozambique. By no coincidence, the Tanzanian ethnic situation is equally unusual. The society contains more than 120 cultural and linguistic minorities, most of which have yet to develop strong communal allegiances. Ninety-nine percent of all Tanzanians are African, and 95 percent are Bantu-speaking. The rest speak Nilotic, Paranilotic, Cushitic, and Khoisan languages. Countering this cultural and linguistic diversity is Kiswahili, which under government sponsorship provides an increasingly effective medium of communication for the entire country. The fifteen largest ethnic groups account for only half the total population, and none is economically or politically dominant. Reflecting the general population distribution, ten of the fifteen largest groups inhabit the densely populated fringes of the country. Even these aggregates are small. The Sukuma, who live south of Lake Victoria, account for only about 13 percent of the population, and no other group exceeds 5 percent.

A fairly representative profile of Tanzanian ethnicity is conveyed in a brief look at the five largest ethnic groups. The Sukuma are a heterogeneous people whose scattered communities were once organized under a series of chiefs, headmen, and more powerful councils of elders. During the colonial period they were administratively centralized and introduced to cotton production. The Sukuma have developed a weak sense of collective identity based primarily on their shared economic interests. Economic issues prompted them to become involved in politics but have never led to the establishment of a forceful ethnic solidarity. Instead, the Sukuma are becoming redivided along economic class lines.

In contrast to the Sukuma, the Makonde of southeastern Tanzania were never fully exposed to the cash economy and today live in physically and culturally isolated settlements on the poorly watered Makonde Plateau. Like other reclusive groups, the Makonde have responded to external socioeconomic and political changes by becoming ethnically more self-conscious and xenophobic.[15]

Among Tanzania's most modernized and economically differentiated societies are the Chagga and Haya of Kilimanjaro and West Lake regions. The Chagga occupy closely spaced homesteads extending outward from the southern slopes of Kilimanjaro, and in precolonial times they were divided into about thirty competitive chiefdoms. The Germans and British consolidated these systems into a few administrative units. They also introduced the Chagga to coffee production and mission education. These innovations enabled the Chagga to adapt themselves to the changing order and to develop an identity defined in terms of their social and economic advantages. Chagga hold a proportion of the positions in the Tanzanian civil service and educational structure much greater than their 4 percent share of the population.[16]

Most of Tanzania's contemporary ethnic groups were traditionally composed of small and democratic kinship societies. These were organized according to extended family and lineage membership and, especially among the pastoralists, also according to age sets. Some traditional societies had chiefs and headmen, whose powers were limited by custom and by the practice of collective decision making. The Haya provide a partial exception to these norms, having developed a limited number of large and hierarchically organized states near the western shore of Lake Victoria. The Haya states were administratively absorbed within the colonial order and offered a comparatively wide range of economic and educational opportunities. Haya farmers cultivated and traded in coffee even before the Europeans arrived and today are about as wealthy and well educated as the northeastern Chagga. Also like the Chagga, many Haya have left their crowded homeland and occupy a demographically disproportionate number of positions in the public sector and educational system.[17]

In much the same manner as the neighboring and culturally related Sukuma, the Nyamwezi of Tabora Region have evolved a shallow ethnic identity based on their common economic interests. Originally living in small and independent chiefdoms, they came under Arab influence during the nineteenth century. One of Zanzibar's major trade routes crossed Nyamwezi country, and the Nyamwezi actively participated in Zanzibari commerce. In spite of their contacts with Arab merchants and their subsequent colonial experiences, however, the Nyamwezi have remained socially fragmented. Whatever unity exists among them derives from their acquired passion for trading.[18]

These cultural vignettes cannot convey the rich social and cultural diversity of Tanzania. They are intended instead to demonstrate that large-scale communalism is not a critical factor in Tanzania. This generalization applies also to Zanzibar, where ethnic animosities of long standing have failed to create a sustained pattern of communal rivalry. Postrevolutionary tensions have in fact declined within the Shirazi community and between it and the more recently settled African groups that still tend to identify with their original mainland cultures.

Ethnic envy exists and sometimes presents political problems. A leading example is the frequently expressed complaint that senior positions in the civil service have been "captured" by the Chagga and Haya. For the most part, however, ethnicity is localistic and passive rather than aggregative and assertive. Throughout Africa, colonialism destroyed the organizational bases of traditional societies. But in Tanzania neither colonialism nor the African reaction to it resulted in a permanent reintegration of these societies into large and communally organized ethnic groups. Julius Nyerere was born a Zanaki. This makes him part of an ethnic community that represents only about one-half of 1 percent of the total population. Nyerere organized TANU not because he was a Zanaki, but because he was a nationalist. Tanzania's real difficulties are imposed not by competitive ethnicity but by the country's cultural fragmentation, basic poverty, and developmentally unsatisfactory human settlement patterns. In these respects the Makonde are more typical than the Chagga.

The Economic Dimension

The Tanzanian economy is predominantly agricultural.[19] In 1979, 54 percent of the country's gross domestic product (GDP) was earned in agricultural production and 22 percent in industrial activity, including mining and agricultural processing. Agriculture employs more than 80 percent of the labor force; industry claims only about 6 percent. Ninety percent of Tanzania's 1978 exports were agricultural primary products, 85 percent of which were sold to industrial countries. These statistics suggest that Tanzania has not yet achieved a diversified economy, but it should at least be able to provide for the subsistence needs of its people. Unfortunately, this last conclusion is incorrect; in the early 1980s Tanzania was economically worse off than at any time since independence and had even to import food.

With an estimated per capita GDP of Shs.2,080 ($260) in 1979, Tanzania ranked as the twenty-ninth poorest of 155 countries surveyed by the World Bank. Moreover, in 1977 the food sector was unable to satisfy more than 89 percent of the society's daily caloric requirements. According to a UN index of per capita food production, the Tanzanian output of staple crops (mainly sorghum and millet, maize, rice, and cassava) dropped by 6 percent between 1969–1971 and 1977–1979. Population growth is responsible to a significant extent for this decline; agricultural production itself grew at an average annual rate of 4.9 percent between 1970 and 1979.

Many of Tanzania's domestic economic problems result from its unfavorable international economic position. Major exports include coffee, cotton, and sisal. World prices for these commodities have declined since the mid-1970s and in the case of sisal, which once earned the largest amount of foreign exchange, the

Figure 2.3. A Farm Family Inspecting Its Cotton Crop. (Courtesy Tanzanian Ministry of Agriculture)

international market began to deteriorate in the middle 1960s. On the other hand, prices for essential imports have increased dramatically since the early 1970s. The costs of imported oil rose from 10 percent of export earnings in 1973 to about 60 percent in 1980, in spite of an average annual reduction in petroleum consumption of 2.9 percent from 1974 to 1979. Drought-related food grain imports consumed another 20 percent of export earnings in 1980 and by 1981 surpassed the 108,000 metric ton annual average established between 1976 and 1978.[20] Despite a determined effort to reduce unnecessary imports, the average volume of imported merchandise decreased by only 0.5 percent annually between 1970 and 1979, while the volume of exports declined at an average annual rate of 6.6 percent. Tanzanian exports were valued at Shs.4.2 billion ($523 million) in 1979, but import costs totaled nearly Shs.8.8 billion ($1.1 billion).

Inflation has worsened this imbalance. In 1980 the real value of Tanzanian imports fell below its 1973 level, and the national inflation rate grew from an annual average of 1.8 percent between 1960 and 1970 to an annual average of 13 percent from 1970 to 1979. The balance-of-payments deficit rose from Shs.203 million ($29 million) in 1970 to a staggering Shs.3.7 billion ($457 million) in 1979, and the external public debt increased from Shs.1.7 billion ($248 million) to Shs.9.2 billion ($1.15 billion). International debt service required 9 percent of export earnings in 1980, yet at Shs.2.3 billion ($286 million), Tanzania's international payments arrears equaled half the value of 1980 exports.

Tourism once represented a fairly lucrative source of foreign excha has suffered from Tanzania's economic policy disputes with Kenya (see Cha ... o). In 1977 these differences caused Tanzania to close its border with Kenya, preventing Nairobi-based tourists from visiting the northern Tanzanian game parks. Park visits declined by nearly 50 percent between 1976 and 1977, from more than 300,000 to about 155,000, and the total number of visitors decreased from about 168,000 to about 118,000. Foreign exchange earnings in the tourist industry fell from Shs.88 million ($11 million) to Shs.73 million ($9 million) during these years. The waning fortunes of the economy have also discouraged tourism, as has domestic uncertainty about the place of free-spending tourists in a country that is trying to overcome grinding poverty.[21] Still, Tanzania maintains international-class hotels, game lodges, and even an international airport near the favorite tourist haunts of Lake Manyara, Ngorongoro Crater, and the Serengeti National Park. Moreover, visits are steadily increasing, from approximately 242,000 bed-nights in 1979 to about 292,000 bed-nights in 1980. No longer able to enjoy the luxuries of Nairobi and also visit the Tanzanian parks, many tourists are opting to spend all their time—and money—in Tanzania. In an interesting departure from the past, a growing number of guests seem less interested in wild game than in the social and cultural aspects of the country.

MEETING THE ECOLOGICAL CHALLENGE

Until well after independence, the vast majority of rural Tanzanians lived on scattered homesteads, not in villages. Even in some of the more heavily populated areas, settlement in villages was discouraged by the low carrying capacity of the land and by a land-tenure system that required the continual subdivision of individual holdings into smaller, less economic, and often widely spaced plots. A dispersed settlement pattern in turn perpetuated extreme cultural pluralism and a lack of occupational specialization. It also weakened the ability of rural dwellers to solve ecological problems through collective action—and thus helps to explain why some Tanzanians still resort to cosmologies involving witchcraft and sorcery[22] and are frequently loath to accept new and therefore risky agricultural practices.

Once independence was achieved, the leadership began searching in earnest for mechanisms through which to create an economically productive and integrated society and a stable and efficient system of representative government. They determined that of the many factors preventing the realization of these goals, the most pressing and yet most approachable had to do with land tenure and use. In appreciating the need for sustained communication with the countryside, the leadership recognized that such contacts could be neither established nor maintained with a society that was so widely dispersed. Julius Nyerere emphasized this point in his first presidential address to parliament.

> The hand hoe will not bring us the things we need today . . . we have got to begin using the plough and the tractor. . . . But we cannot even do this if our people . . . continue living scattered over a wide area, far apart from each other. . . . The first and absolutely essential thing to do, therefore, . . . is to begin living in proper villages. [In political terms] the growth of village life will help us in improving our system of

democratic government. It is true that at present both the Central Government and
our Local Government bodies are elected by democratic methods. But, although the
methods may be democratic, the operation of democracy is not yet what it should be,
nor can it be while the majority of our rural population remains so widely scattered.[23]

In short, organized village communities were viewed as essential to political integration and economic development in a culturally diverse and impoverished
society.

3

The Ambiguities of
Independence

IN SEARCH OF A POLITICAL FORMULA

At independence, Tanganyika's political elites were singularly unprepared to deal with the policy problems that were heaped upon them by the departing colonial regime and by the pluralistic, unintegrated, and demographically changing society over which they now ruled. In particular, the TANU nationalists were not ready to build a nation in the manner envisioned by party President Julius Nyerere. The nation-building issue and Nyerere's evolving philosophy on how best to resolve it form two threads that run continuously through Tanzanian politics. In a real sense, much of the postcolonial political experience can be interpreted as a series of attempted reconciliations between the moral thought of Nyerere and the difficult and frequently conflicting realities of his country. The successes and failures of these attempts contribute an important chapter to the annals of twentieth-century political development. In the first five years of independence, Tanganyikans devised three distinct formulas for a well-ordered and integrated political system. The subsequent interplay of these designs continues heavily to influence the Tanzanian political process, and the period of their delineation is of seminal importance to the contemporary national scene.

The Colonial Formula

The first formula was a British-inspired independence strategy upon which the TANU leadership initially felt compelled to agree. Had it been followed for long, this plan would have indefinitely perpetuated Tanganyikan dependence on Britain and guaranteed the further development of a racially and socioeconomically stratified class system. The British formula for independence included six major propositions, which can be summarized as follows.[1]

1. Because of the extreme shortage of professionally trained Africans, senior civil service posts should be filled by expatriate officers until fully qualified Tanganyikans became available.
2. Because of the technical complexities of the tasks involved, and in keeping with the principle of civil service neutrality that was inherited with

41

independence, oversight of the policy process should be entrusted to the cabinet and parliament, but policies themselves should be made and executed by the politically disinterested—and of course expatriate-led—civil service.

3. Because of the country's strained financial resources and economically marginal hinterlands, development programs should be conservatively planned and applied primarily in behalf of those who were most likely to profit from them. Specifically, the 1961–1964 colonial development plan, with its cautious "improvement approach" to agricultural development and its emphasis on only the most "progressive" (i.e., economically productive) farmers,[2] should be adopted by the independent government.

4. To compensate for its lack of funds and qualified personnel, the government should encourage foreign and domestic private investment in Tanganyika and provide guaranteed support for private manufacturing and commercial activities.

5. To ensure their continued participation in Tanganyika's economic development, the resident European and Asian minorities should be allowed to retain their economic advantages over the African majority, if not the social and economic hegemony they enjoyed during the colonial period.

6. To facilitate an orderly transition to modernity, TANU should play two roles. First, it should protect the European and Asian minorities from economically and racially motivated harassment by the African community. Second, it should mobilize popular support for a developmental program that promised an unequal distribution of immediate benefits. These assignments would reduce TANU to "converting the mass participation which it had secured in the independence struggle into a government-directed national development effort."[3]

Objectively speaking, these arguments had much to recommend them. Independence had been achieved, but the colonial legacies of inadequate financial and human resources remained. The only way out seemed to lie in a temporary reliance on the colonial administrative and economic relationshps already in place. But these arrangements were strongly opposed by TANU nationalists and the people at large. The most visible aspects of this dilemma were the continuation of British colonial officers in senior central and local government positions and a trade sector still dominated by Asians.

By 1961 only 547 of about 4,000 middle- and higher-level government posts were held by Africans, and little provision had been made for educating enough Tanganyikans to reverse this imbalance.[4] In an October 1960 address to the preindependence parliament, Nyerere outlined a stopgap approach to the Africanization of the civil service.

> First, it will remain the policy of the Government that every vacancy arising in the civil service should, if possible, be filled by an appointment made locally and

that recourse should only be had to recruitment from outside East Africa if no suitable candidate (of any race) can be found locally. That is our first principle.

Secondly, within this policy, in the case of new appointments to the service, it is Government's intention that African candidates of Tanganyika should have prior claim to consideration.

Thirdly, only if no suitable, qualified Tanganyika African candidate is available should other candidates be considered.[5]

In compromises such as these, Nyerere found himself isolated from his political base. TANU regulars were clamoring for government jobs, desired access to private economic rewards, and had issues to settle with European district administrators and African native authorities. Nyerere was also disturbed that the logic of events conflicted fundamentally with his personal views on racial and socioeconomic equality, domestic and international dependency, and the proper locus of ultimate authority in a democratic nation-state. Finally, he had become increasingly worried by a tendency for his TANU followers to look only to him for political guidance and, paradoxically, by the scrambling of many TANU functionaries for positions of wealth, status, and power. Nyerere decided to resign from the prime ministership and, as president of TANU, to devote his full attention to the intellectual and organizational problems of building a political order based on the ideals of African economic independence, democracy, equality, and service to the common good. He published four papers on these subjects during 1962, soon after he left the government in January.[6] The ideas expressed in these and other documents reflect the moral basis of Nyerere's blueprint for a future Tanzania.

The Nyerere Formula

The political thought of Julius Nyerere bears a greater resemblance to the consensual and organic notions of Jean Jacques Rousseau than to the competitive and contractual model of John Locke. Although the writings of these and other Europeans influenced Nyerere's contemplations, the core of his philosophical reasoning derives from the customs and practices of traditional Africa. In trying to find a political formula that was unique to his part of the world, Nyerere looked to the small and kinship-based societies of the precolonial past. In the African versions of equality, democracy, and socialism, he found traditional consistencies that in his judgment could be adapted to serve the collective needs of the present.

Equality. It is a common belief in traditional subsistence societies that the human environment contains a fixed, and usually scarce, quantity of resources that constitute the necessities of life. According to this cosmology, one person or group can acquire a surplus of these necessities only at the expense of another person or group. Because of their harsh physical surroundings, labor-intensive technologies, and familial social organizations, traditional cultures placed a high survival value on the equal sharing of resources. In view of the disastrous practical consequences of inequality, Nyerere noted,

the different shares of different members of the family unit can never get very unequal; all the customs operate to bring them constantly back towards equality. And it would certainly be a major social disgrace for one member of a family, however senior, to be acquiring, for example, personal property in the form of trade, clothes, or anything else while another member was denied his basic rights.[7]

The emphasis here is on the kinship unit; unavoidable inequalities could and did exist among different descent groups. But the colonial experience joined many of these local societies into a new and broader set of relationships. It also introduced social and economic inequalities and a spirit of interpersonal and intergroup competitiveness. These aspects of colonialism conflict with the egalitarian social imperative and make it difficult for Africans to practice it in the much larger fellowship of which they are now members. Unless the alien constraints are removed, the new society can never develop the necessary moral foundation. Without it, Nyerere wrote, "It is then impossible for all members of the society to discuss together as equals with a common interest in the maintenance and development of society. The common interest has been at least partially replaced by two interests, those of the 'haves' and those of the 'have-nots.' The unity of society has been weakened because the equality of its members has been broken."[8]

The rhetoric of racial and socioeconomic equality has often appeared in anticolonial protest statements, but it has frequently been contradicted in the treatment of the former colonial elites after independence. On the pressing issue of race, Nyerere stated his own intentions in 1959: "I say again to my friends the non-Africans in East Africa, that when we say we want to establish the rights of individuals in our countries, irrespective of race, we mean it."[9] He demonstrated this commitment in 1961 when he strongly and successfully opposed a TANU parliamentary attempt to limit postindependence citizenship to Tanganyika Africans.

Nyerere's year away from government enabled him to think more generally about the moral problems of independence. In 1962, he firmly reestablished the traditional conception of equality as one of the guiding principles of an independent Tanganyika.

> In no state is there enough wealth to satisfy the desire of a single individual for power and prestige. Consequently, the moment wealth is divorced from its purpose, which is the banishment of poverty, there develops a ruthless competition between individuals; each person tries to get more wealth, simply so that he will have more power, and more prestige, than his fellows. Wealth becomes an instrument of domination, a means of humiliating other people.[10]

The answer to this morally unacceptable condition is social and economic equality, which is possible only through democracy and socialism.

Democracy. Consistently with his belief in equality, Nyerere rejected elitism in any form. Even in socially and economically stratified societies, "history has shown very clearly that it is when the wealthy and educated minority mistrusts the poor and the uneducated majority that the menace of totalitarianism threatens a state, not when that wealthy and educated minority trusts the majority."[11] He accepted that there could be no substitute for majority rule but denied that the only way to achieve democracy is through the clash of competing interests. In January 1963 Nyerere published the pamphlet *Democracy and the Party System*,[12] in which he summarized his earlier thinking on the subject[13] and instructed TANU in the meaning and obligations of democracy in its Tanganyikan idiom. The pamphlet took as its theme Guy Clutton-Brock's aphorism on African village politics: "The Elders sit under a big tree, and talk until they agree."

Nyerere had previously expressed his antipathy to competitive party politics in essentially apologetic terms. He argued that countries like Tanganyika could not yet afford the risks of adopting Western democratic forms. Europe had taken centuries to achieve the levels of social integration and economic development necessary to permit the establishment of both popular representation and governmental stability through institutionalized political conflict. As independence approached, Nyerere began to search for a more positive rationale to acknowledge the immediate need for political unity and stability without sacrificing representative democracy in the process. For inspiration he again turned to the values and customs of traditional Africa.

Nyerere advanced an ideal conception of small and well-integrated societies in which private interests are routinely subordinated to common goals. Of necessity and by choice, consensus prevails over dissension in all spheres of public life. In the political systems of such societies, "the traditional method of conducting affairs is by free discussion."[14] Colonialism created the need for African political consensus on a much larger scale, and for a single oppositional movement quite unlike the party organizations of Britain.

> We . . . did not build TANU to oppose the Conservative Party of England, or to support the Labour Party! The divisions of English politicians meant nothing to us. As far as we were concerned they were all colonialists, and we built up TANU as a national movement to rid ourselves of their colonialism. A Tanganyikan who helped the imperialists was regarded as a traitor to his country, not as a believer in "Two-Party" democracy![15]

Terminating the colonial relationship removed the need to contend over fundamental goals, which to Nyerere provided the only legitimate, albeit unfortunate, reason for party competition in other countries. In Tanganyika, TANU represented a nascent social order in which there already existed basic agreement on what had to be accomplished—the elimination of ignorance, poverty, and disease. Differing methods might be proposed to attain these ends, and some leaders might be more effective than others. But if participation in TANU remained open to all citizens and if this participation resulted in the free expression of ideas and selection of leaders at all levels, representative democracy would be achieved and the wasteful and traditionally alien distinction between politics and government would be erased. "There would be no need to hold one set of elections within the party, and another set afterwards for the public. All elections would be equally open to everybody . . . and the present distinction between TANU and the TANU Government—a distinction which, as a matter of fact, our people do not in the least understand—would vanish."[16] So too would disappear the divisive and dangerous separation of administrators from the political process, which the British justified by the myth of civil service neutrality.

> Furthermore, there would be no need to continue with the present artificial distinc-
> tion between politicians and civil servants — a distinction desirable only in the context
> of a multi-party system where the continuity of public administration must not be
> thrown out of gear at every switch from one "party" government to another. For,
> once you begin to think in terms of a single national movement instead of a number
> of rival factional parties, it becomes absurd to exclude a whole group of the most in-
> telligent and able members of the community from participation in the discussion of
> policy simply because they happen to be civil servants.[17]

Widespread popular agreement on the underlying purposes of society offers an opportunity for unity and stability through the representative deliberations of a freely elected party-government. Underlying this agreement is a common belief in economic equality and, more important, social worth.

Socialism. Nyerere has devoted much of his recent thought and writing to the problem of creating socialism in Tanzania. His views on this subject were less fully elaborated in 1962 than were his ideas on equality and democracy. Never-theless, in "Ujamaa — The Basis of African Socialism," he presented a uniquely African conception of socialism that was intended to provide a moral justification for economic equality and democratic political participation. This abstraction has come to form the core of Tanzania's developmental ideology.

It may be that part of the reason why Tanzania remains financially less sol-vent than other African countries is that the Tanzanian developmental strategy reflects a philosophical orientation that is moral rather than material. In em-phasizing that "socialism, like democracy, is an attitude of mind,"[18] Nyerere separated himself from the empirical socialism of Europe and turned to the essen-tial purpose of economic activity in precolonial Africa — to provide for the welfare of all, not to enrich the acquisitive or even the hardworking.

For Nyerere, the difference between these motivations was also the dif-ference between the foreign and fundamentally "antisocial" economic systems in-troduced by the Germans and the British and the indigenous practice of *ujamaa* (literally, "familyhood"). In its economic application, *ujamaa* signifies the equal sharing of benefits according to need and, of course, willingness to work. This concept is crucial to Nyerere's later thinking, and to political and economic rela-tions in modern Tanzania:

> Apart from the anti-social effects of the accumulation of personal wealth, the very
> desire to accumulate it must be interpreted as a vote of "no confidence" in the social
> system. For when a society is so organized that it cares about its individuals, then,
> provided he is willing to work, no individual within that society should worry about
> what will happen to him tomorrow if he does not hoard wealth today. Society itself
> should look after him, or his widow, or his orphans. This is exactly what traditional
> African society succeeded in doing. Both the "rich" and the "poor" individual were
> completely secure in African society. Natural catastrophe brought famine, but it
> brought famine to everybody — "poor" or "rich." Nobody starved, either of food or of

Figure 3.1. President Nyerere (center) Tilling His Ancestral Land near Butiama, Mara Region. (Courtesy Tanzanian Ministry of Agriculture)

human dignity, because he lacked personal wealth; he could depend on the wealth possessed by the community of which he was a member. There can be no such thing as acquisitive socialism.[19]

Without the impediment of a class system, which had not yet formed in Tanganyika, a socially responsible political leadership could employ the *ujamaa* concept to create a moral society in place of the moral societies that were destroyed by colonialism.[20] The vehicle for *ujamaa* applied nationally would, in Nyerere's words, be "a strong political organization active in every village, which acts like a two way all-weather road along which the purposes, plans and problems of Government travel to the people at the same time as the ideas, desires and misunderstandings of the people can travel direct to the Government. This is the job of the new TANU."[21] If TANU could fill this role, economic equality and political democracy would follow.

Morally informed discussion formed the basis of Nyerere's formula for independence, which was soon to be organizationally applied and tested in the crucible of practical politics. But even as Nyerere wrote and taught about his vision of a moral and socially responsible Tanganyika, another formula was being shaped in the practical political arena.

The Kawawa Formula

Nyerere resigned from government to pursue the philosophical and educational tasks of party reform. In January 1962 he placed Rashidi Kawawa in charge of reforming the government. As a TANU leader and trade union organizer during the 1950s, Kawawa was one of Nyerere's closest associates. Before 1962 he served as TANU vice-president, minister for local government, and minister without portfolio. After he became prime minister, Kawawa again demonstrated his talent for consolidating power by distributing rewards and punishments. Unhampered by Nyerere's normative and practical concerns, Kawawa proceeded immediately to appoint TANU militants to cabinet, subcabinet, and senior civil service positions. He also replaced expatriate provincial and district commissioners with local party leaders, whose assignments as regional and area commissioners now included political mobilization as well as administration.

Turning to the labor movement, Kawawa settled a festering dispute between his old faction, which supported the TANU emphasis on production, and a second group, which argued in favor of increased wages and fringe benefits. Kawawa appointed the leader of his adversaries, Christopher Tumbo, as Tanganyikan high commissioner to London and made his own man, Michael Kamaliza, minister for health and labor. Legislation was passed restricting the right to strike, prohibiting senior civil servants from joining unions, and requiring all trade unions to affiliate with Kawawa's Tanganyika Federation of Labour (TFL). These laws were followed by the Preventive Detention Act, which gave the national executive sweeping powers of preventive detention. These new laws clearly signaled the government's intention to eliminate factional politics and organized expressions of economic discontent. Kawawa sought to sweeten this pill by raising the official minimum wage. As a result, average monthly earnings increased from Shs.96 ($13.70) to Shs.165 ($23.50) between 1961 and 1963.[22]

Kawawa's greatest challenge lay in the Africanization of the civil service. He approached this issue by supporting in-service training, commissioning a study of higher-level job priorities in relation to the supply of school leavers and university graduates,[23] and increasing the number of local government posts to lessen the complexity of individual positions. Approximately 660 Africans were added to the civil service during 1962, and about 260 non-Africans were removed. These were small numbers, but they represented a new direction in staffing policy. In its 1963 report, the newly appointed Africanisation Commission promised that although expatriates would continue to be required in order to implement the national development plan, "this does not mean that the Government has relaxed in the slightest degree its determination to accelerate, by all means at its command, the development of Tanganyikans to man the national Civil Service."[24]

Kawawa advanced yet another political formula for independence, one aimed at strengthening TANU's oligarchic control over the public and private sectors. Although he remained personally loyal to Nyerere, his long-term goals were in basic disagreement with Nyerere's plan for the future. Kawawa's policies reflected "fairly typical expressions of the aspirations of a new political class, an African elite whose claim to status and power rested upon its political power. . . . The government of Tanganyika in 1962 was still a government without a consciously articulated ideology. It had not embraced Nyerere's egalitarian concerns nor did it seriously move in a socialist direction in its economic policies."[25]

The Kawawa government introduced a republican constitution that took effect on December 9, 1962, following a national election. Nyerere campaigned for the office of president and won by an overwhelming majority. Kawawa was made vice-president, ensuring that his political approach would continue to be influential.

THE POLITICS OF UNCERTAINTY

None of Tanganyika's three independence formulas could be easily dismissed. To a very large extent they represented competing but equivalent requirements. The British plan stressed administrative efficiency, economic stability, and the importance of external resources. Nyerere's idealism emphasized popular participation and, through it, self-reliant socioeconomic and political integration. The Kawawa initiatives underlined the need for a disciplined political organization to provide the leadership required for national unification and mass compliance with development programs. In attempting to satisfy the immediate need for an official policy line, the TANU party-government was confronted by a series of difficult choices among these requirements. As Nyerere later observed, "We have to make choices between good things, not between good things and bad things: to plan means to choose."[26] The period of choosing was marked by ideological inconsistencies and conflicting practical results and was punctuated by a succession of domestic and international crises. It was not until 1967 that a coherent and durable political strategy emerged. This strategy remains explicitly committed to Nyerere's goals for Tanzania, but its implementation has raised dissonant issues that first appeared in the British and Kawawa formulas for independence, were further shaped in the politics of 1963 through 1966, and have since become permanent features of the Tanzanian political landscape.

Political Uncertainty on the Domestic Front

From the standpoint of most ordinary Tanganyikans, the simple issue of national independence had turned into a confusing proposition. On the one hand, the people were urged toward democratic political participation, common ownership of the means of production, and an equal distribution of economic rewards. On the other hand, both the party and the government were becoming increasingly centralized and authoritarian, and the country's developmental investments and patterns of economic benefit still clearly favored the small minority of "progressive" farmers, urban wage earners, and non-African entrepreneurs.

In 1962 and again in 1965, the TANU constitution was amended to promote democratic and socialist values. Between these years, a system of popularly elected village development committees and ten-house party cells was instituted to serve as the first section of Nyerere's "two way all-weather road" linking the political and administrative center with its rural and urban periphery.[27] But it became clear at the outset that these structures were intended more to provide central access to the localities than to encourage local participation in central policymaking. In response to directives incessantly exhorting farmers and other workers to engage in self-help activities, development committees and TANU cells began demanding the major improvements in living standards that had been promised before independence. Both messages went largely unheeded.

Table 3.1 suggests that by the time of independence, African producers had considerably expanded their role in Tanganyika's agricultural economy. The most impressive economic gains had been made by the "progressive" Chagga, Haya, and Sukuma growers of northeastern and western Tanganyika. Under a policy that encouraged agricultural development through the further improvement of already productive cash-crop areas, highly unequal rural income distributions persisted well into the 1960s. Although not as serious as in other developing countries, significant disparities also existed between rural and urban incomes. In 1964, the average cash earnings of rural Africans were approximately Shs.121 ($17) per month; urban African earnings averaged about Shs.211 ($30).[28]

Inequality and alienation were reinforced by a policy drift toward the British approach to development and by Rashidi Kawawa's oligarchic conception of political organization. The first trend is illustrated in one of the most important rural development efforts of the early 1960s, the village settlement program.[29]

Village Settlement. Tanganyika faced one of its greatest developmental problems in the physical dispersal of its rural population. President Nyerere considered this problem to be sufficiently serious to make it a major topic of his inaugural address to parliament. The response was immediate. Anticipating an outpouring of financial and technical assistance, farmers and townspeople rushed to form more than 300 villages by early 1964. In an attempt to control this enthusiasm, the

TABLE 3.1

Tanzania's Three Principal Export Crops, 1948 and 1961

Crop	Type of Production	1948	(Shs.)ᵃ	1961
Sisal Fiber	Mostly European	178,600,000		280,560,000
Cotton	Entirely African	25,560,000		135,880,000
Coffee	Mostly African	17,940,000		135,240,000

Source: Tanganyika, Fact Sheet, Section 4 (Dar es Salaam: Tanganyika Information Services, 1963), p. 1.

ᵃDuring this period, one U.S. dollar equalled about seven Tanganyikan shillings.

cabinet-level Rural Settlement Commission was established in 1963.[30] The commission was authorized to approve plans for new settlements and to allocate domestic and foreign aid funds in support of approved projects.

The president instructed the Rural Settlement Commission to approve only settlement projects that offered their participants an opportunity to become economically self-sufficient in the shortest possible time. Under its enabling legislation, the commission appointed an executive Village Settlement Agency, whose senior positions were filled entirely by European expatriates. On the basis of feasibility studies prepared by Israeli consultants, the agency developed a plan for a few experimental villages. The plan provided for up to ten pilot village settlements funded entirely from foreign aid sources and relied on economic incentives to attract settlers.

Each community would consist of about 250 families located on 0.4-hectare (1-acre) homestead plots, with the surrounding land reserved for communally organized and mechanically assisted cash-crop production. About Shs.3 million ($430,000) was allocated for the establishment of each pilot settlement. This amount was extremely high by Tanganyikan standards for the assistance of so few people, but the settlers were required to repay Shs.2.7 million ($386,000) over a twenty-five-year period. Cash crops were to be planted immediately, so that repayment installments could begin within two or three years. To justify the financial risks involved, the Village Settlement Agency recommended that only skilled farmers be recruited as settlers and that professional managers be employed as village overseers. One of the managers' lesser assignments was to help prepare the villagers to run their own communities as democratically representative cooperative societies. Like the senior agency staff, all the first managers were expatriates.

The village settlement program became a centerpiece of Tanzania's first five-year plan[31] and heralded a shift in policy emphasis from rural "improvement" to "transformation." Fewer than twenty settlements were begun between 1964 and 1966. None fulfilled the unrealistic production and repayment schedules, nor did any show much prospect of evolving into self-reliant village democracies. By 1965, President Nyerere began to express serious doubts about a rural development program that was so heavily capitalized, was funded and managed by expatriates, and produced little more than a heightened sense of dependency among its beneficiaries: "We have learned a number of lessons from this early experience. In particular we intend to reduce the capitalisation of these villages. To burden the farmer with very heavy debts at the outset, and at the same time, to make it appear that Government can provide all services, is not the best way of promoting activity. . . . The individual no less than the nation must learn the lesson of greater self-reliance."[32]

In April 1966, Vice-President Kawawa announced Nyerere's decision to discontinue the village settlement program and to invest the remaining funds in less intensive but more extensive assistance to existing rural communities. This decision was reached mainly because the settlers showed "far less enthusiasm and are less hard-working than 'settlers' in 'spontaneous' and unassisted [rural development] schemes."[33] The village settlement program had proved an expensive failure and reflected the political uncertainty that at this time permeated the entire policy process. Had it been continued, the program would have accomplished exactly the opposite of what Nyerere intended: It would have subjected the country's rural development goals to the approval of foreign aid donors and the operational decisions of expatriate technicians; it would have fed the prevalent conception that leadership and economic rewards originated in Dar es Salaam and not through local exertion; and it would have given official support to the evolution of a rural class system dominated by a small number of publicly subsidized cash-crop farmers. Seeing these dangers, Nyerere ended the program even before he had something with which to replace it.

Army Mutiny and the Union with Zanzibar. Nyerere and his colleagues had little time for development planning during 1964 and 1965 because of several political crises. The Zanzibari revolution took place in January 1964 and triggered a series of events that by April had led to Tanganyika's uneasy union with Zanzibar and Pemba. From January 16 to 20, soldiers of the 1st Battalion, Tanganyika Rifles, mutinied in an attempt to force the government to raise their pay and replace their British officers with Africans. The mutiny caused Nyerere to flee Dar es Salaam and very nearly brought down the government. British troops were required to suppress it.

After his return and following the merger, Nyerere discovered that neither he nor TANU enjoyed much influence over Zanzibar. The unification had been approved by the Zanzibari Revolutionary Council and by the Tanganyikan National Assembly. Zanzibari President Abeid Karume was demoted to first vice-president of the United Republic and placed in charge of Zanzibari affairs, and Rashidi Kawawa was appointed second vice-president with executive jurisdiction over the mainland. In spite of these formal provisions, the Zanzibari ministries and ruling Afro-Shirazi Party remained essentially autonomous and continued to control many responsibilities normally reserved for sovereign governments. These included supervision of Zanzibar's army, its immigration and emigration services, and its foreign exchange reserves. Most important, the Afro-Shirazi Party did not merge with TANU as had been hoped. Through its representatives on the Revolutionary Council, the ASP began conducting its own foreign relations with several states, including the German Democratic Republic. This step jeopardized mainland Tanzania's important economic relations with the German Federal Republic.

One-Party Oligarchy or One-Party Democracy? These crises, combined with TANU's increasing loss of rural support, demonstrated that neither the party nor the government was fully in control of the Tanzanian political process. The mainland leadership responded by employing the Preventive Detention Act and subsequent legislation to arrest TANU critics in the trade unions, suspected participants in the mutiny, and local residents who were generally considered by their regional and area commissioners to be political malcontents. Several hundred people had been detained by the early part of 1965.

The events of 1964 also stimulated members of the political elite to demand the legalization of the one-party state. Led by TANU Secretary General Oscar Kambona, party militants argued that in the interests of domestic security, competitive elections were an undesirable—and, in any case, an unnecessary—component of single-party rule. Nyerere agreed with the establishment of a one-party state but insisted on fair and open elections. Pulling back from his reluctant acceptance of the earlier detentions, he expressed grave concern over the elite's inclination to treat all political criticism as subversive. Faced with this threat to the realization of his moral society, Nyerere temporarily ignored the problems of Zanzibar and the need for a viable development policy and instead concentrated his attention on the twin issues of party stability and democratic reform.

In order first to confirm TANU's political supremacy, the private trade unions and cooperative societies were amalgamated into the National Union of Tanganyika Workers (NUTA) and the Cooperative Union of Tanzania (CUT). These organizations were formally affiliated with TANU and required to adopt a productionist policy orientation. Nyerere's goal was not to stifle opposition but to confine it within the ideological parameters and decision-making processes of the party. The only difficulty was that while Nyerere determined the ideology, routine decision making remained in the hands of the TANU oligarchy, which had now consolidated its hold on the trade union and cooperative movements.

Reforms in local government were only slightly more democratic. The colonial native authorities were abolished in 1963 and their duties taken over by district councils. These bodies were elected but not autonomous. Their bylaws had to be approved by the minister for local government, and their financial estimates were screened by the regional commissioners under whose jurisdictions they operated. Administrative controls did not prevent some councils from trying to separate themselves from local TANU policies. In a few of the economically most prosperous districts, council seats were won by party defectors. To forestall further desertions while retaining representative local government, district TANU organizations were empowered to approve all candidates for district council seats.

Councillors were further required to participate in annual district party conferences and to accept as their district council chairmen local TANU chairmen. The opportunity was also taken to strengthen the party in the villages. Membership on village development committees, which had previously been determined by open election, was now limited to TANU ten-house cell leaders. These changes all but fused TANU and local government organizations. The process was completed in 1972, when all local government bodies were eliminated and their functions assumed by the regional governments under party scrutiny.

Nyerere's vision of a one-party democracy was rapidly becoming eclipsed by the party's progressive eradication of meaningful opposition. In January 1963, the TANU National Executive Committee determined that the Tanganyikan constitution should be rewritten to acknowledge the country's one-party government. The committee reluctantly authorized Nyerere to establish a presidential commission to investigate and make recommendations on the requirements for a one-party democracy. The commission was appointed in January of the following year and published its recommendations in 1965.[34] These suggestions were modified by the ASP and TANU executive committees[35] and then incorporated into the Interim Constitution of 1965, which remained in force until 1977.[36] The democratic reforms of the new constitution were embodied in procedures governing election to the National Assembly.

In summary, TANU was to remain a mass party and any member could be nominated to stand for election to parliament if he or she could obtain the support of twenty-five electors. The party's annual district conferences would interview all prospective candidates and rank their preferences. The TANU National Executive Committee would then decide on two candidates for each constituency. It could overrule the priorities suggested by the district conferences, but for only the most compelling reasons.

No candidate was permitted to spend personal funds to advance his or her candidacy. All campaign events were to be organized by the district TANU committees and were required to include both candidates in each constituency. No candidate was allowed to campaign nationally, to use only a locally spoken language in public statements and debates, or to make any appeal based on racial, ethnic, or religious considerations.

In an effort to make the National Assembly as broadly representative as possible, a number of additional members would be selected by the elected constituency representatives from nomination lists submitted by national organizations, such as NUTA, CUT, and the University of Dar es Salaam. Still other nominations would be made by the president, with a share reserved for candidates from Zanzibar. All regional commissioners and a portion of the Zanzibar Revolutionary Council were also included as members of the National Assembly. These provisions were intended to preserve party unity, prevent voting along racial and ethnic lines, and still ensure that a true cross section of the pluralistic Tanzanian society was represented at the highest governmental level.

The system's first test came in the national election of September 1965.[37] Single candidates ran in only 6 of the 107 constituencies. Thirty-one incumbent members of parliament decided not to run and twelve failed to be nominated by their district TANU conferences or the National Executive Committee. Seventeen other incumbents lost their seats in the voting, including two ministers and six junior ministers. The 1965 election demonstrated that intraparty electoral competition could effectively provide leadership opportunities for ambitious TANU members and thus help open the party to new political talent and public scrutiny. The problem was that ultimate power did not reside in the National Assembly, whose members were confined mainly to approving policies decided upon by the TANU elite and explaining these policies to local constituents. Symbolic of the National Assembly's continued subservience to the party oligarchy, soon after the election an act was passed extending to the TANU National Executive Committee the parliamentary right to summon witnesses and subpoena evidence.[38]

This unstable mixture of democracy and authoritarianism was paralleled by the equally incongruous coexistence of an egalitarian ideology and an emerging class system favoring party and government employees, privileged racial minorities, urban wage earners, and successful cash-crop farmers.[39] These inconsistencies were exacerbated by Tanzania's increasing dependence on foreign aid, which compromised even TANU's political autonomy and conflicted with Nyerere's insistence on national self-determination and his growing interest in economic self-reliance at all levels. Tanzania's domestic political uncertainty originated to a significant extent in the unfavorable foreign policy environment of the early 1960s.

Political Uncertainty in Foreign Policy

In a speech before the 1963 Afro-Asian Solidarity Conference, Nyerere reflected on the fragility of independence and what he called the "second scramble" for Africa: "This Second Scramble will be conducted in a different manner from the first, but its purpose will be the same—to get control of our continent. . . . Neither should we allow ourselves to think of this new imperialism solely in terms of the old colonial powers. Imperialism is a by-product of wealth and power; we have to be on guard against incursions by any one."[40] As he spoke, a five-year development plan was being formulated that was to depend on the recruitment of skilled expatriates and on the availability of funds contributed by Britain and other countries. Between 1964 and 1966, Nyerere's rhetoric was to find concrete examples in the dependency relationship linking Tanzania with its major trading partners and aid donors.

Of the 1964-1965 Tanzanian development budget, 83 percent was to come from foreign loans and grants, and only 17 percent was obtainable from domestic sources.[41] The three largest sources of foreign aid were Britain, the United States, and the Federal Republic of Germany. These countries had together supplied almost 90 percent of the meager Shs.299 million ($43 million) received since independence, but a series of foreign policy crises endangered further relations with each.

Tanzania and Britain. When Rhodesia's white minority unilaterally declared its independence on November 11, 1965, the Organization of African Unity demanded that Britain end the rebellion by December 15. Already angered by

Britain's close ties with the racist Republic of South Africa, Nyerere broke off diplomatic and economic relations when the British failed to meet this deadline. If only temporarily, Tanzania rejected the help of its former colonial power, which since 1961 had furnished nearly 70 percent of all financial aid and was about to provide a loan of Shs.40 million ($5.71 million) that was considered essential to the fulfillment of the 1964–1969 development plan.

Tanzania and the United States. To Nyerere, racism and foreign intervention in internal affairs constituted fundamental threats to human dignity and national independence and were therefore not susceptible to political compromise. This belief induced him to make Dar es Salaam the headquarters for a number of exile groups seeking the liberation of Mozambique, Rhodesia (now Zimbabwe), South West Africa (Namibia), and South Africa. It also caused him pointedly to criticize U.S. economic involvement in southern Africa and U.S. military intervention in Vietnam, the Dominican Republic, and the Congo (now Zaire). The United States in turn expressed displeasure at what it interpreted as Tanzanian support for leftist-inspired political instability in southern Africa.

Tanzanian-American relations became particularly strained in November 1964, when Foreign Minister Oscar Kambona released documents alleging that there had been a plot by the United States to overthrow President Nyerere and his government. Although the U.S. State Department was able easily to demonstrate that the documents were forgeries, Kambona had made the allegation a cause célèbre. Nyerere dismissed the charge but, in deference to Kambona, stopped far short of offering an apology to the United States. To make matters worse, in January 1975 Tanzania expelled two U.S. diplomats whom Abeid Karume had accused of plotting the overthrow of the Zanzibari government. Although this charge was also proved absurd, Nyerere was compelled to acknowledge it. Washington recalled its ambassador and held in abeyance aid negotiations then in progress. Nyerere then recalled the Tanzanian ambassador to the United States, interrupting official contact with a government that since 1961 had supplied nearly 11 percent of Tanganyika's overseas development funds.

Tanzania and West Germany. In his speech asking parliament to ratify the articles of union between Tanganyika and Zanzibar, President Nyerere anticipated a conflict that would shortly alienate Tanzania's third most important foreign aid donor.

> The Union between Tanganyika and Zanzibar has been determined by our two governments for the interests of Africa and African unity. There is no other reason. Unity in our continent does not have to come via Moscow or Washington. It is an insult to Africa to read cold war politics into every move towards African Unity. Africa has its own maturity and its own will. Our Unity is inspired by a very simple ideology—Unity. We do not propose this Union in order to support any of the "isms" of this world.[42]

If Nyerere seems to protest too much here, it is because from the beginning cold war politics engulfed the union. Even before independence, Babu and his Umma party had maintained close ties with Cuba and the People's Republic of China. The left wing of the Afro-Shirazi Party looked to Moscow for its postindependence support. Under the openly suspicious scrutiny of the United States and Britain, Cuba and the socialist states of Eastern Europe and Asia quickly recognized Zanzibar's revolutionary government and began immediately to send it military and developmental assistance. The hastily conceived union prevented further growth of this dependency relationship between Zanzibar and the Eastern bloc countries, but it failed to extract Tanzania from its uncomfortable position in the middle of both the East-West confrontation and the Sino-Soviet dispute. The issue came to a head in 1964.

East Germany had been the first state to recognize the revolutionary government of Zanzibar and was soon engaged in building a powerful radio transmitter, a hospital, and urban housing in Zanzibar town. West Germany was training mainland naval and air force officers, had already provided Tanganyika with about Shs.78.75 million ($11.25 million) in agricultural and urban housing assistance, and was committed to health and educational projects worth another Shs.70 million ($10 million). With the unification of the mainland and the islands, West Germany's Hallstein Doctrine—under which the Federal Republic could not extend diplomatic recognition to any country maintaining official relations with East Germany—became applicable to its relations with Tanzania. President Nyerere tried to solve the problem by ordering that all diplomatic missions on Zanzibar be reduced to consular status, but this directive was ignored by the East Germans as well as the Zanzibaris. The West German government rejected a Tanzanian compromise proposal that an East German consul general's office be established in Dar es Salaam. Indignant at this intrusion of the cold war into Tanzanian domestic affiairs, Nyerere allowed the office to be created, and the West Germans promptly withdrew their military training staff. Tanzania responded by ordering the withdrawal of all official West German technical assistance. As a matter of principle and practical concession to the Zanzibaris, Nyerere was compelled to refuse the badly needed services and financial contributions of a friendly nation that had provided nearly 9 percent of all external funding received since independence.

The foreign policy crises of 1964 and 1965 underlined Tanzania's unavoidable dependence on foreign assistance and revealed the dangers of accepting this help from only a few sources. By 1966, the party-government had taken steps to diversify its sources of aid, but not to reduce the size of its total aid package. Sweden, Canada, the Netherlands, and Denmark quickly stepped in to compensate for the loss of British and German resources, and cooperative agreements were concluded with the People's Republic of China on several major projects, including a rail link with Zambia. But the basic purposes and ideal levels of foreign aid, as well as the domestic goals foreign aid was intended to serve, had not yet been determined. It *had* become increasingly clear from the domestic and international events of the early independence years that the politics of uncertainty had to end.

4

Toward Socialism and Democracy

In his recent critique of Tanzanian development policy, Reginald Herbold Green identified an important premise of the new political approach that was selected in 1967:

> the belief that concentration of effort and the creation of a new situation are often critical to securing broad breakthroughs. Bureaucracies normally administer what exists and make marginal changes within it much more readily than they devise major changes. In this, the Tanzanian bureaucracy is no exception. On the other hand, once major changes are ordered, some civil servants, managers, and planners are quite able to devise responsive and creative ways to promote these changes because they accept the new guidelines as changing the terms of reference within which they operate.[1]

The first such change, and the one that has most influenced subsequent innovations, was prescribed in a TANU declaration announced at Arusha in February 1967. The theme of this document is *ujamaa na kujitegemea*—socialism and self-reliance.

The Arusha Declaration

With its heavy dependence on foreign economic assistance, its increasing elitism, and the emerging class structure it fostered in both rural and urban areas, the postindependence political system was rapidly moving Tanzania away from Julius Nyerere's vision of an egalitarian and democratic society. His reaction was to draft a policy statement in which he reiterated the basic principles of his political formula for independence and then restated them in the form of specific guidelines for a transition to democratic socialism.

In its final version, the Arusha Declaration attacked incipient class formation from a distinctly non-Marxist perspective.

> We can put the capitalists and feudalists on one side and the farmers and workers on the other. But we can also divide the people into urban dwellers on the one side and those who live in the rural areas on the other. If we are not careful we might get to the

59

position where the real exploitation in Tanzania is that of the town dwellers exploiting the peasants.[2]

To Nyerere, exploitation and national economic dependency are both worsened
by a premature commitment to industrial programs that emphasize import
substitution, borrow foreign exchange but earn none in return, and therefore fail
even to repay their costs. Early industrialization perpetuates neocolonial subservience to other countries and in various ways taxes farmers to pay for the
establishment of urban manufacturing centers. The result is a widening gap, over
which the country has little control, between urban and rural standards of living.
For these reasons, the declaration stipulated that the Tanzanian approach to
socialism should discourage private foreign investment and industrialization and
concentrate on labor-intensive agricultural development. "Industries will come
and money will come but their foundation is *the people* and their *hard work*,
especially in AGRICULTURE. This is the meaning of self-reliance."[3] Self-reliant
agriculture would also reduce Tanzania's addiction to money in general and
"humanitarian" foreign aid in particular and thereby inhibit the growth of an internationally subsidized rural class system.

Nyerere freely acknowledged that a long-term dedication to material
sacrifice and self-help could not be sustained without a fresh injection of creative
and persuasive political leadership. He continued to reject the notion that this
catalyst should be supplied by an elite vanguard party whose ideological
evangelists were rigorously schooled in the organizational and motivational
precepts of "scientific" socialism.[4] He held to his original belief that while TANU
should persevere in guiding and overseeing the government and society, it should
also remain a mass party. The only change would be that instead of being open to
all Tanzanians, TANU membership would be limited to those who were willing to
accept the hardships of social and economic leveling and the delays of achieving
modernity through democratic discussion and rural self-reliance. These requirements applied especially to the party and government professionals, who
would no longer be permitted to advance themselves while the majority of people
suffered in abject poverty.

In order to curb the further development of an acquisitive elite, the Arusha
Declaration set forth a stringent leadership code:

1. Every TANU and Government leader must be either a peasant or a worker, and
   should in no way be associated with the practices of capitalism or feudalism.
2. No TANU or Government leader should hold shares in any company.
3. No TANU or Government leader should hold directorships in any privately
   owned enterprise.
4. No TANU or Government leader should receive two or more salaries.
5. No TANU or Government leader should own houses which he rents to others.[5]

The leadership category was very broadly defined to include middle- and higher-
level civil servants, elected representatives, and senior officials of the party, its

affiliated organizations, and government corporations. To prevent intrafamilial subterfuges, the code was applied to the spouses of leaders as well.

On the day after the declaration was promulgated, the government began gaining control over the "commanding heights" of the economy by nationalizing the banks and the major food-processing, insurance, and export trading companies. These actions were widely supported, but the leadership code caused immediate and widespread objection within the party and bureaucracy. Leaders were allowed to convert their assets into trust funds for their children and to employ hired labor on their farms. In spite of these concessions and the party's formal approval of the declaration as a whole, the leadership code was neither well supported nor extensively followed in the first few years.[6] It lacked any enforcement provisions and was more and more openly ignored, until in 1973 the TANU National Executive Committee instructed the National Assembly to establish an enforcement committee. Similar units were added to the senior police commissioner's office and to the prime minister's office, which had recently been formed to administer regional and local government. These controversies were accompanied by attempts by a dissident faction in the National Assembly to resist legislative instructions from the party. TANU responded oligarchically by expelling the dissidents from parliament and by publishing a new set of guidelines (the *Mwongozo*) that asserted party supremacy over both the government and the economy.

In his 1962 statement that "socialism, like democracy, is an attitude of mind," Nyerere recognized the psychological difficulty of eradicating the avaricious and authoritarian inclinations of Tanzania's political class. These temptations persisted in post-Arusha Tanzania. "In very human terms," according to one observer, "the problem is one of convincing leaders not to act in what they see as their own self-interest."[7] Alternative goals and rewards were clearly needed to stimulate the cooperation of both elites and masses and thus to overcome poverty's intrinsic capacity to produce extreme economic inequality and highly centralized accumulations of power.

Expanding Participation: The Decentralization Policy

By the end of 1971, the only real achievement of the Arusha Declaration was the nationalization of Tanzania's major industrial and commercial enterprises.[8] Having gained the "commanding heights" of the economy in support of national self-reliance, Nyerere focused the country's attention on the construction of a democratic and socialist political system.

> The purpose of both the Arusha Declaration and of Mwongozo was to give the people power over their own lives and their own development. We have made great progress in seizing power from the hands of capitalists and traditionalists, but we must face the fact that, to the mass of people, power is still something wielded by others—even if on their behalf.[9]

To counter the increasing centralization of government and to encourage greater popular participation in the planning and implementation of development projects, Nyerere sponsored legislation that in 1972 transferred considerable authority from the central government to the localities.[10] Under the decentralization

Figure 4.1. District Headquarters, Musoma.

policy, the number of regions and districts was increased to provide smaller and
more manageable local administrative units. Greater autonomy was also extended
to regional and area commissioners, who were now made responsible to the prime
minister's office and were afforded the assistance of newly appointed regional and
district development directors. The development directors were placed in charge
of technical specialists organized into regional and district development teams.
These teams were intended to incorporate the central administrators and technicians who had individually handled such important policy areas as agriculture,
health, and education.

Mass participation was to be ensured through a series of local advisory committees, which were intended to make suggestions to the partly elected district
development councils and wholly appointed regional development committees.
Under the leadership of their commissioners and development directors, these
higher-level bodies were to devise annual development plans and submit them for
approval to the district and regional TANU executive committees. The regional
TANU committees would then transmit the plans to the relevant central agencies
for final approval and funding. All existing local government organizations were
abolished in favor of this new system, which placed primary decision-making
power in the hands of the regional and area commissioners and the regional and
district development directors.

The decentralization policy was reinforced by an existing program, included
in the 1969–1974 development plan, to transfer certain productive activities from
Dar es Salaam to eight regional cities slated for planned expansion. In November
1974 it was announced that the national capital itself would be moved to
Dodoma. The intent was to bring the party-government closer to the majority of

people and to aid in the development of impoverished Dodoma Region. If it is ever completed, the new capital will be physically dispersed. This will accentuate the Arusha Declaration's philosophical commitment to agriculture and self-help by providing spaces where farming as well as business, industry, and government can be carried on. The Dodoma building project was scheduled for completion in 1990, but by the early 1980s work had fallen far behind schedule because of insufficient funds and the unavailability of construction materials. A certain amount of decentralization was achieved by the relocation of the party headquarters and prime minister's office at Dodoma; but the national capital project had also fallen behind in its scheduled transfer of central government ministries from Dar es Salaam.

Administrative efficiency and sensitivity to local needs may have been enhanced through decentralization, but democratic participation suffered in the process. Development funds and scarce technical expertise continued to be allocated by the central government, and what vestiges of local self-determination had existed were now virtually eliminated in a system that confined local residents to a purely advisory role. Matters were not improved by the advisory committees' unfamiliarity with integrated development planning or by their propensity to avoid self-help recommendations and to demand expensive benefits such as schools and medical dispensaries.

The new arrangements succeeded in decentralizing administration but failed to expand participation beyond the electoral opportunities that had been successfully tested in 1965 and again in 1970. These elections had allowed Tanzanians to register their dissatisfaction with the government's marginal performance in raising their standard of living. In the 1970 election, more than half the parliamentarians who sought reelection were either not renominated by their district party conferences or defeated at the polls.[11] Partly in response to the economic conditions that had influenced these results, a revolutionary rural development program was implemented to create self-reliant socialism in an administratively decentralized Tanzania. This program was launched under the policy of *ujamaa vijijini* ("socialist villages").

Transforming the Human Environment: Villagization

President Nyerere had no intention of returning to the capital-intensive and now defunct village settlement experiment, but he remained convinced that rural development could not be accomplished in the absence of well-organized villages. In late 1967 he again called upon farmers to form such communities, but this time to increase their productivity and welfare through collective self-help. By 1974, however, only about 8 percent of the villages established since 1967 had advanced to the stage of fully communal production and income distribution.[12] More important, less than one-fifth of the rural population was living in villages large enough to permit collectivization without sacrificing crop yields. It was evident that before rural dwellers could be convinced to work together and share equally in the rewards, they would first have to begin living together on a much larger scale.

The leadership conceded that in order to facilitate quick improvements in productivity and welfare, cooperative working relationships would have to be temporarily accepted in place of the collectivist blueprint for *ujamaa* socialism. These arrangements reflected grassroots conditions, traditions, and opinion. They would become progressively eliminated under the guidance of recently strengthened local party and government organizations, once the majority of the rural population had been relocated into villages. Reasoning in this way, TANU and the government effectively committed themselves to villagization without socialism.[13]

The Villages and *Ujamaa* Villages Act of 1975 gave legal recognition to this policy line.[14] Any group of no fewer than 250 households may seek recognition as an incorporated village. Once registered, the community also serves as a multipurpose cooperative society that, unlike under previous regulations, can obtain investment credit before achieving socialist modes of production and distribution. When the party regional executive committee decides that most of the village's productive and distributive functions are being performed communally, it may recommend that the prime minister's office designate the hamlet an *ujamaa* village. *Ujamaa* status entitles the community to receive increased developmental assistance from the central and regional governments.

These provisions embody a degree of voluntarism that was not always present in the effort to create socialist villages. Under the personal guidance of President Nyerere and Prime Minister Rashidi Kawawa, three resettlement techniques had been employed in the decade after 1967. Until 1970, voluntary compliance was sought on a locally selective basis, combined with compulsory "operations"[15] in Rufiji and Handeni districts to mitigate the effects of flooding and drought. From 1970 until the end of 1973, the selective persuasion campaign was replaced by a "frontal approach" of inducing as many people as possible to move into *ujamaa* villages, with the promise of financial and technical assistance resources as rewards. Several new operations were also mounted during this period, some by local party-government zealots and others by administrators who were hoping to ease the effects of localized drought conditions. After 1973, under Operation Tanzania, exhortation and inducement were supplemented by a willingness to use force in support of rapid villagization throughout the mainland.

The results were dramatic. In 1970, 531,000 Tanzanians, less than 5 percent of the mainland population, were living in 1,956 villages. These villages had an average occupancy of 271 people. By 1974, following the persuasion and inducement campaigns and after several local operations, the villagized population had grown to about 2,028,000 – 14 percent of the total population – living in 5,628 settlements with an average membership of 360. After the first full year of compulsion, the number of villagers stood at about 9,150,000, or 60 percent of the mainland population, residing in about 6,400 villages with an average occupancy of 1,430. And at the conclusion of Operation Tanzania in 1977, an estimated 79 percent of the 1978 mainland population and 85 percent of all rural dwellers – more than 13 million people – was living in 7,300 villages with an average membership of about 1,849.[16]

As Table 4.1 indicates, the impact of this huge exercise in directed migration was not felt equally in all regions. By 1975, 70 percent of the population that would eventually be villagized was settled into 6,384 villages at an average occupancy of 1,289 inhabitants per community. A disquieting pattern emerges when

Figure 4.2. *Ujamaa* Village Elders. (Courtesy Tanzanian Ministry of Agriculture)

the regions are assembled according to their villagization statistics and the rainfall probability rankings introduced in Chapter 2. In the eight least and marginally well-watered regions, about 63 percent of their combined 1978 populations were resettled into 2,992 villages, with an average membership of 1,416 people per village. The ten moderately well-watered regions accounted for only slightly more than one million more settlers than were relocated in the low rainfall group. A

TABLE 4.1

The Villagization of Mainland Tanzania

Region	Population Relocated by 1975	Share of 1978 Regional Population (%)	Number of Villages in 1975	Average Village Population in 1975
		Least Well-Watered		
Mtwara	667,413	86.5	773	863
Rukwa	346,800	76.7	385	900
Shinyanga	940,335	71.0	369	2,540
Tabora	553,770	67.7	324	1,708
Lindi	386,664	73.2	315	1,196
		Marginally Well-Watered		
Dodoma	630,858	65.0	388	1,634
Singida	247,834	40.4	258	960
Arusha	275,765	29.7	180	1,532

		Moderately Well-Watered		
Mwanza	1,437,095	99.6	106	2,371
Iringa	804,391	87.2	464	1,876
Mbeya	934,800	86.5	933	1,000
Tanga	105,184	10.1	302	348
Morogoro	123,256	13.1	397	521
Dar es Salaam	40,000	4.7	53	800
Mara	626,687	86.6	303	2,232
Kigoma	452,285	69.7	193	2,343
Ruvuma	378,511	67.1	315	1,201
Coast	157,641	30.5	238	528
		Most Well-Watered		
Kilimanjaro	14,508	1.6	16	281
West Lake	26,432	2.6	72	957

Source: Tanzania, Maendeleo ya Vijiji vya Ujamaa (Dar es Salaam: Prime Minister's Office, 1975), reproduced in Adolpho Mascarenhas, "After Villagization - What?" in Bismarck U. Mwansasu and Cranford Pratt (eds.), Towards Socialism in Tanzania (Toronto: University of Toronto Press, 1979), pp. 152-54.

smaller percentage of these regions' populations was placed into fewer villages with a lower average rate of occupancy. The two best-watered mainland regions were virtually untouched by Operation Tanzania. Only 1.6 and 2.6 percent of their populations were resettled into a total of 88 villages with an average membership of 619. Conversely, of the twelve regions with more than 60 percent of their populations villagized, six (Mtwara, Rukwa, Shinyanga, Tabora, Lindi, and Dodoma) have chronic rainfall problems and one (Mwanza) experiences frequent difficulties because of its low rainfall in relation to its small geographical area, large number of residents, and heavy rural population densities. If Mwanza is placed in the low rainfall group, 60 percent of the people who were uprooted and resettled by 1975 lived in regions where rainfall-related ecological crises are the most likely.

Several factors help to explain these demographic variations between the less and more well-watered regions. The latter group is less villagized partly because it contains some of Tanzania's most heavily urbanized regions, such as Dar es Salaam, Tanga, West Lake, and Morogoro. As will be seen, Operation Tanzania drew many fewer people from the cities than from the countryside. Mountainous areas were also avoided in Operation Tanzania, because of their already high population densities and because of the permanent tree crops that grow in the highlands.[17] In addition to an unwillingness to risk agricultural production losses in the more prosperous regions, the party and government shared a political reason to direct their zeal elsewhere. As they sought to fill their resettlement quotas, local officials exploited the tendency for poorer farmers to resist villagization less than richer farmers. For whatever reasons, regions least able to provide for their residents are among the most extensively villagized.

Encouraging people to work together has generally proved to be much more difficult than getting them to live together, partly because of the settlers' unwillingness to organize themselves collectively. From the party's failure to come forth with an ideologically acceptable and yet economically workable alternative, Mascarenhas concluded that "resettlement was adopted as a technocratic solution to development, creating an atmosphere in which it was assumed that the only thing necessary was to put people in villages."[18] This assumption has helped to produce a series of economic catastrophes (see Chapter 5). From the political standpoint of creating self-reliant *ujamaa* villages, the program was stillborn.

Operation Tanzania included a pilot program to villagize some 15,000 jobless residents of Dar es Salaam. In an effort to stem migration to the capital city and to enforce a party directive that *kile mtu afanye kazi* ("every person must work"), an operation was begun during June 1976 to move the unemployed into more than thirty new villages. The resettlement sites were all located in the rural portions of Ilala, Temeke, and Kinondoni districts, which together form Dar es Salaam Region. By September, local TANU officials had identified about 11,000 jobless, representing less than 2 percent of Dar es Salaam's regional population.

From the beginning, the scheme was administratively cumbersome, expensive, and unpopular with the city's residents. Cooperation among the responsible party and government agencies was difficult. It was also discovered that not enough funds and building materials were available to construct the necessary village housing. Worst of all, Dar es Salaam's unemployed simply refused to be moved voluntarily. By November, fewer than 150 people had reported to their district party offices for resettlement. On November 17, the regional TANU secretary, Joseph Rwegasira, announced that compulsion would henceforth be used to carry out what had come to be called Operation Rwegasira. "Since they have refused to move voluntarily we have now decided to look for them. . . . We will go to every ward leader, ten cell leader, and land lord to look for those who have refused to respond to the call for moving to the villages and engag[ing] in productive work."[19] A plan was devised whereby 1,000 people from each district would be moved at ten-day intervals until all were relocated by year's end. Established urban residents would be taken to the nearby villages and more recent migrants repatriated to their home districts. A series of police "swoops" followed, which netted not only the jobless but also visitors to the city, workers without their identity cards, and even housewives.

It immediately became apparent that the resettlement and repatriation campaign was suffering the same fate that had befallen earlier "roundups" conducted by the colonial authorities in 1957 and the independent government in 1964. Within a few days, most of the reluctant pioneers had filtered back into the city. Policy changes to salvage the operation were considered, including the criminal arrest of "stubborn jobless persons who will try to reduce this task to a joke."[20] But an unfortunate parallel had already been discovered between the urban and rural resettlement programs. Operation Rwegasira had been devised as a "technocratic solution" to the problems of urban unemployment and was not accompanied by a serious effort to provide gainful employment for the new villagers. The operation was subjected to unusually open criticism in the official press and then quietly dropped.

The villagization program failed to produce local self-reliance and democratic socialism. The party and bureaucracy had resorted to private economic incentives and compulsion in order to accelerate the rural revolution. Even these expedients had failed, and food production dropped precipitously. In 1970, Tanzania had exported a maize surplus of 540,000 tons. By 1974, the country was forced to import 400,000 tons of food grains, including 300,000 tons of maize.[21] Between 1970 and 1975 total per capita food production fell to its 1960 level.[22] This led to considerable political discontent in both the rural and urban areas. In the 1975 parliamentary election, two ministers and twenty-one other incumbents out of a total of ninety-six lost their seats.

If local democracy and self-reliance were negatively influenced by villagization, so too was Nyerere's goal of reducing Tanzanian dependence on foreign aid. Bowing to pressures exerted by multilateral and bilateral assistance agencies, ministerial officials agreed to "a tacit understanding that policies to restore a high level of agricultural production should take precedence over policies oriented towards the fulfillment of normative social goals."[23] Food production was an especially worthy objective, but the circumstances under which it was reasserted also reinforced Tanzania's subservience to a number of donor governments and international development organizations.

Villagization created more problems than it solved. It also illustrated TANU's growing reliance on coercive and somewhat frantic "operations," inspired by Rashidi Kawawa, among others, as an instrument of political reform and economic development. Operations Tanzania and Rwegasira were accompanied by "anticapitalist" and "antielitist" policy offensives that summarily abolished most private medical practice, dismissed 9,500 officials—or nearly 20 percent of all public service employees—and suddenly closed hundreds of private shops because of their "unfair" competition with widely scattered retail government cooperatives.[24]

The operations reflected a tactic favored by the TANU oligarchy, "in which an impossible goal is announced for achievement tomorrow, and from which results not the full accomplishment of the stated aims but probably more progress than would have been possible had the implementation process been much more bureaucratic and orderly."[25] In practice, this approach squared well with Kawawa's political formula for independence, rendered Nyerere's formula increasingly problematic, and left open the questions of the locus, direction, and purposes of political authority in Tanzania. The massive political and governmental reorganizations of 1976 and 1977 offered partial responses to these questions.

FORMING A NEW PARTY-GOVERNMENT

Post-Arusha politics were further complicated by a new set of international problems (see Chapters 5 and 6) and by the mainland's continuing inability to attain political and economic unification with Zanzibar. The Zanzibari question is best understood in relation to the successes of the Arusha Declaration and the incentives they provided for further political innovation.

The Achievements of Arusha

Tanzanians celebrated the tenth anniversary of the Arusha Declaration on February 5, 1977. In his anniversary speech, President Nyerere recounted the failures and triumphs of the first decade of commitment to *ujamaa na kujitegemea*.[26] He admitted that Tanzania was neither socialist nor self-reliant, that its democratic processes were still flawed by elitism and coercion, and that economic exploitation and inequality still existed. He also expressed concern that economic growth was lagging behind its pre-Arusha levels. The national income increased at an average annual rate of 6.4 percent from 1964 to 1967, but it dropped to an average increase of only 4.2 percent between 1967 and 1975. Part of the problem was that government had become the fastest-growing sector of the economy. Nonproductive administrative costs had risen from 10.9 percent of the national income in 1967 to 16 percent in 1975. This increase resulted from an unchanged official preference for large and managerially top-heavy development projects, combined with bureaucratic job creation, inefficiency, and widespread delinquencies in debt repayment by local government agencies and *ujamaa* villages.

The achievements of Arusha were to be found not in the objective performances of the polity and economy, but rather in the subjective reorientation of society toward socialism and equality. The drift toward a highly stratified class system had been halted, and gross economic inequalities were no longer present in a system that had gained control of the major means of production and income

Figure 4.3. Women Drawing Water from an Improved Village Tap, Ruvuma Region. (Courtesy Tanzanian Ministry of Agriculture)

distribution. The ratio between the highest and lowest government salaries had been reduced from seventy to one in 1961 to about fifteen to one in 1975, on the way to an estimated six to one in 1980.[27] Progress had also been made in providing basic health and educational opportunities for all Tanzanians. By 1978, 7.7 million rural residents enjoyed easy access to piped water; half the almost 8,000 villages had dispensaries; and nearly 950,000 children had entered primary school—twice as many as in 1967. Most important to Nyerere, a pronounced moral shift was occurring in the society, away from norms encouraging acquisitiveness and self-seeking and toward those favoring cooperation and collective advancement. This change was symbolized by Tanzanians' swift and universal adoption of *ndugu* ("comrade") in place of *bwana* ("mister") and *bibi* ("miss" and "Mrs.") in personal references to themselves and to foreigners whom they considered supportive of Tanzania's socialist aspirations.

Nyerere concluded that the real accomplishments of the preceding ten years lay in the intellectual and material foundations that had been established for socialism, but that were threatened by flagging economic growth and by the shortcomings of an only half-committed political leadership. In the troubled rural areas, for example,

the real failure seems to have been a lack of political leadership and technical understanding at the village and district level. Despite the call in "Politics is

Figure 4.4. *Siasa Ni Kilimo* ("Politics Is Agriculture"). President Nyerere (left, kneeling) Visiting a Village Farm. (Courtesy of Tanzanian Ministry of Agriculture)

Agriculture" for all political leaders to learn the basics of good husbandry in their areas, and to join with peasants in production, we have continued to shout at the peasants and exhort them to produce more, without doing much to help them or to work with them in a relationship of mutual respect.[28]

To Nyerere, such failings were serious but correctable through a rejuvenation of the party and government.

One unsolved problem was the role of Zanzibar in Tanzanian political and economic development. In 1975 the TANU leadership instructed that the Interim Constitution be amended to confirm the party as the highest policymaking authority for the mainland. Formal party supremacy was established in 1977 by a permanent constitution that was adopted after the Chama cha Mapinduzi had been formed to replace TANU and Zanzibar's Afro-Shirazi Party. Following these basic structural changes, Zanzibar could at last be included in the movement toward democracy and socialism.

The Political Opening of Zanzibar

Abeid Karume was assassinated in April 1972 and replaced by Aboud Jumbe. Karume had been a xenophobic and repressive ruler and had effectively prevented the economic and political integration of Zanzibar with the mainland. He and Julius Nyerere had rarely agreed on the legitimate methods and goals of government; but Nyerere had had no choice but to tolerate Karume's penchant for forced-labor brigades, his fondness for "people's courts" and the death penalty in dealing with real and imagined political enemies, and his refusal to invest even a portion of the islands' sizable clove profits in development projects. Nyerere had also been unable to convince Karume that international nonalignment meant a willingness to maintain friendly relations with many governments and not just with those representing the communist states of Eastern Europe and Asia.

Jumbe was in much closer agreement with the strategies and objectives of mainland Tanzania. Two years older than Nyerere, he had also studied at Uganda's Makerere College and earned an education diploma in 1945. For the next fourteen years, he worked as a teacher on Zanzibar. Jumbe became politically active in the early 1950s, helping to organize the short-lived Zanzibar National Union. He retired from his educational career in 1960 to help lead the Afro-Shirazi Party. After the revolution and union with Tanganyika, Jumbe quietly served as minister for health and social insurance and then as minister of state in the first vice-president's office. This position placed him directly under Karume.

Soon after becoming head of the Afro-Shirazi Party and Zanzibari government, Jumbe directed that one-third of the Shs.840 million ($120 million) annual clove proceeds be devoted to rural and urban development. He also gradually opened trade and aid negotiations with several Western governments. Jumbe eased political censorship and reduced oppression by eliminating forced labor. He also influenced the commutation of death sentences for all but seven of thirty-seven alleged conspirators in the Karume assassination.

The most important difference between Karume and his successor was that Jumbe wished to further the union with Tanganyika and thereby expand his

Figure 4.5. Vice-President Jumbe (left, shaking hands) Talking with the Elders of Mjimwema *Ujamaa* Village. (Courtesy Tanzanian Ministry of Agriculture)

personal constituency to include the mainland as well as the islands. He eagerly consented when Nyerere suggested that a referendum be held among TANU and ASP members on a merger of the two parties. The referendum was conducted in 1975, and its results were encouraging to both leaders. Of 6,389 TANU branches, only 6 opposed the merger. All of ASP's 257 branches approved of the proposed reorganization.[29] A joint commission was formed to draft a new party constitution, and Nyerere insisted that the commission aim for nothing less than a total melding of the existing parties into a single movement. The resulting document was ratified by both national party conferences on January 21, 1977. Thus was born the Chama cha Mapinduzi (CCM, or Revolutionary party), opening the present phase of Tanzanian political development.[30]

CCM: A New Beginning or Old Wine in New Bottles?

In his Arusha Day speech, President Nyerere made it clear that the CCM represented a joining of two political parties and not two governments. For the time being at least, Zanzibar would retain its Revolutionary Council, a separate House of Representatives, and several semiautonomous ministries.

The CCM constitution itself draws heavily on the past and again commits Tanzania to socialism and self-reliance as "the only way of building a society of free and equal citizens."[31] Party structures at all levels are patterned after those of

TANU.[32] Ten-house cells are designated for the rural areas and fifty-member cells for places of work, each with an elected leader. Branch organizations include monthly general meetings, representative annual conferences, and executive committees led by elected chairmen and appointed secretaries. District and regional units consist of conferences held at thirty-month intervals, executive and working committees, and chairmen and secretaries. At the central level, a national conference serves as the party's highest decision-making authority and in an election year nominates a candidate for the presidency of Tanzania. Policies are suggested to the conference by a national executive committee and smaller central committee which also oversee policy implementation. The CCM is headed by a chairman and vice-chairman elected by the national conference. Routine party administration is supervised by a chief executive secretary assisted by two deputies. The party includes an elders' section and five "mass organizations" representing youth, women, parents, the national trade union, and the cooperative movement.

Like TANU before it, the CCM is one of Africa's most powerful and comprehensively organized political parties. In light of its ideological and organizational links with the past, one may ask what is new about the CCM to justify the recreation of Tanzania's supreme political institution.

All former members of TANU and the ASP automatically belong to the CCM, but new members must enroll in a course of study on party goals and policies and then formally apply for membership. Applicants must also affirm their allegiance to the party constitution, which extends the Arusha Declaration's leadership code to all members. These provisions require a positive act of commitment and conform with Nyerere's wish that party membership be limited to energetic supporters of socialism and equality.

The real break with the past involves the party electoral process and representation in the national government, both of which draw the mainland and Zanzibar into a much closer political relationship than was previously possible. In January 1977 Nyerere and Jumbe were elected CCM chairman and vice-chairman. Nyerere then appointed district and regional party secretaries, and elections were held throughout the year to select other party officials at all levels.

While the party elections were in progress, the National Assembly approved a permanent Tanzanian constitution to replace the Interim Constitution of 1965. The new basic law asserts single-party supremacy over the entire country, but it also recognizes Zanzibar's special status by maintaining its Revolutionary Council and authorizing a separate cabinet and ministerial system for the islands. Governmental integration is promoted through legislative and executive representation. The number of elected parliamentary seats was increased to provide Zanzibar with ten constituency representatives. These seats were promptly filled in the election of December 18, 1977. The constitution also provides for a national executive consisting of a president and only one vice-president, with the understanding that these positions must at all times be shared between a mainlander and a Zanzibari.

CCM Chairman Nyerere and Vice-Chairman Jumbe were appointed president and vice-president until the first all-union election scheduled for 1980. Nyerere took this opportunity to change incumbents in the government's third-ranking office, demoting Rashidi Kawawa from prime minister to minister for defense. Kawawa had been widely criticized for the degree of force employed in the villagization operation and had been faulted even more for his role in the arbitrary closing of small shops. Nyerere was determined to avoid similar economic failures and displays of authoritarianism in the new party-government. Kawawa was replaced by Edward Sokoine, a young civil servant with a reputation for leadership, professional discipline, and technical efficiency. Sokoine's elevation to the prime ministership reinforced a basic policy reorientation. The new concept rejects development administration through enforced political mobilization. It also postpones indefinitely the transition to socialism and instead revives the technocratic spirit of the postindependence British plan for political and economic modernization. The Nyerere formula for building democracy and socialism has been challenged by a different but no less familiar and formidable counterstrategy.

Trends in the Politics of Ujamaa

These tensions among necessary but conflicting approaches to government and development are present in every sector of public life.

The Rural Sector. On September 21, 1977, Prime Minister Sokoine delivered a major policy address at the Kivukoni Ideological College. He outlined a new series of directives, including one allowing each village to set its own pace in creating socialist institutions and processes.[33] Sokoine had already taken steps to stimulate rural productivity and, at the same time, to reduce the power of party officers at the village level. On May 9, 1977, he had directed that by June 1, technical officers should move from the comfort of their district field offices to the villages. The plan was for them to work in the villages from Monday through Thursday of each week and spend Friday and Saturday back at headquarters catching up on their paperwork. The decision affected 7,600 specialists in agriculture, livestock production, forestry, and fisheries.[34] Some of these officers immediately complained that they were not provided with "nights out" allowances, to which Sokoine replied that village service was an integral part of their jobs and therefore not susceptible to further subsidy.

In subsequent decisions Sokoine clearly selected technocratic solutions to the organizational and economic problems of the villages. The World Bank–supported Village Management Training Program was begun in 1976. This project involved the training of one specialist in accounting and practical economics for each of the country's 2,000 wards, each ward consisting of about five villages. Progress was slow, and by mid-1977 only 604 village management technicians were in place. Impatient with these results, Sokoine ordered the immediate reassignment of 8,000 young technicians from the central government ministries to the villages. Four thousand civil servants were selected by December and scheduled to depart for their village posts.

In his Arusha Day speech eleven months earlier, Nyerere had warned against depending too much on technical personnel to advance rural socialism and self-reliance: "These people are not an integral part of the village, affected personally by its success or failure. Therefore, although it is necessary now to give the villages the help of trained government employees, eventually our aim should be to phase these out and gradually replace them by members of the villages who are paid out of village income."[35] By 1980, programs were under way to train villagers to perform technical and managerial functions, but policy still relied on a nation-wide application of the approach to village leadership that was originally adopted in the village settlement program of nearly twenty years ago. This approach was later rejected in favor of local self-help and Nyerere's goal of *ujamaa na kujitegemea*. Rural socialism and self-reliance had again taken a back seat to increased produc-tivity and national income generation.

The Private Economic Sector. In October 1977, Nyerere himself announced that small-scale private industry would once more be encouraged in Tanzania in order to raise productivity, encourage local investment, and ease the managerial burden on an already overworked bureaucracy. The twenty-six companies of the Dar es Salaam Chamber of Commerce responded with plans to invest Shs.121 million ($15 million) in industrial development, the first such commitment of private funds since the nationalizations of 1967. The economy's "commanding heights" were to remain nationalized and the Arusha Declaration's leadership code was still in effect, but a certain amount of socioeconomic inequality was to be tolerated for the sake of economic growth and administrative efficiency.

The Public Sector. One reason Nyerere felt compelled to reinvigorate the private economy was that public-sector performance had sunk to a dangerous low. Disciplinary committees were established at all work places in 1978 in an attempt to curb slackness and accelerate production. Finance Minister Amir Jamal later disclosed to parliament that between 1978 and 1979, Shs.31.56 million ($3.94 million) was lost because of financial mismanagement and supervisory ineffi-ciency.[36] The party-government has been able neither to increase productivity nor to stem a wave of public-sector job creation.

Tanzania experienced extensive flooding in 1979 and a severe drought in 1980. The floods caused widespread crop damage and bridge destruction. The drought forced the government to import nearly 140,000 tons of food grain from the United States at a projected cost of Shs.209 million ($26 million).[37] These natural calamities have been worsened by a near-100 percent increase in petroleum prices since 1979 and by the short but costly war with Uganda (see Chapter 6), which consumed about Shs.4 billion ($500 million) between 1978 and 1980. These unrelenting financial disasters significantly increased Tanzania's foreign aid de-pendence. Annual aid contributions approached $700 million in 1981, represent-ing the highest per capita outlay in tropical Africa and nearly 70 percent of Tan-zania's new developmental investments. To a very large extent, the country's future development will be determined by the actions of more than a dozen bilateral and multilateral donors.

Facing the 1980s

The quest for socialism and democracy continues. Tanzania entered the 1980s in the midst of an unprecedented economic crisis. On the positive side, Tan-zanians have created the potential for a physically and politically better structured society and have achieved a remarkably stable and representative government. In October 1980 the first all-union election was held. Seven million citizens registered for this election, 4 million more than for the first national election of 1965.

Approximately 85 percent of all registered voters went to the polls to select a president and 111 members of the National Assembly.

Julius Nyerere was reelected president with a 93 percent "yes" vote,[38] but more than half the assembly was ousted as an apparent protest against the country's economic difficulties. Zanzibaris overwhelmingly confirmed Aboud Jumbe as president of Zanzibar, chairman of the Revolutionary Council, and vice-president of the United Republic.[39] Edward Sokoine ran unopposed for his National Assembly seat and was reappointed prime minister. He fell ill, however, and was replaced by a fellow economic development specialist, Cleopa Msuya, who had been minister for finance and later for industries. Eleven other ministers were returned to parliament, but one was soon relieved of his ministerial duties in another of Nyerere's increasingly frequent cabinet reshuffles. In January 1981 Nyerere fired the minister for communications and transport, Augustine Mwingira, for financial and managerial improprieties. Party secretaries were replaced in six mainland regions, and 102 Zanzibari civil servants were suspended for violating the Arusha leadership code by taking private part-time jobs.[40] These and more recent personnel changes underline the preoccupation with bureaucratic honesty and performance in the early 1980s.

Strengthened by its fresh popular mandate, a shifting but coherent leadership again faces the challenges of building a socialist and democratic Tanzania. Politicians and administrators realize only too well that their collective success and personal careers both depend on how well they come to grips with a number of hard economic issues.

5

Toward Socialism and Self-Reliance

IN SEARCH OF AN ECONOMIC STRATEGY

Until the Arusha Declaration, Tanzanian development policies encouraged extensive private investment and large financial contributions from abroad. These orientations were in keeping with the macroeconomic premises of the First Development Decade, which the United Nations declared in 1960. The strategy of the time assumed that postcolonial modernization would follow paths that had already been traversed by the industrial and postindustrial societies, whose obligation it now was to help the less developed countries in their transitions to modernity. Tanzania fully accepted this reasoning in its first five-year plan.

The First Five-Year Plan

The Tanzanian economy is not unique among poor countries. It is dominated by a marginally productive agricultural sector, which employs more than 80 percent of the work force yet is unable to generate enough surplus to accelerate growth through a widespread diversification of productive activity. The first five-year plan (1964–1969) sought to transform the economy by attracting private investment and foreign assistance for capital-intensive manufacturing, agricultural, and infrastructural projects.[1] In a speech introducing the plan, President Nyerere confessed that "in the public and private sectors together we are proposing to spend £246 million on development in the next five years—about fifty million pounds a year. Of this, more than half will have to come from outside Tanganyika."[2]

The plan's productive goals were not achieved, partly because of such uncontrollable factors as unexpectedly high population increases, inclement weather conditions, falling export prices, and shortfalls in anticipated foreign aid and investment. Data were also lacking to measure economic performance, so that ill-conceived projects like the village settlement program were blindly implemented until their futility finally became apparent. The plan projected a 6.7 percent annual increase in gross domestic product (GDP). By the end of the planning period, the GDP had risen at an average rate of only 5.3 percent.[3] More seriously, the plan led Tanzania in directions that Nyerere wanted to avoid. Agricultural employ-

79

ment actually declined, and the income gap widened between urban wage earners and small farmers. Economic growth was confined largely to the small industrial sector, which Nyerere considered to be increasingly exploitative. Public spending relied on a steady flow of foreign aid. This support was obtained at a political cost that in some cases became unbearable.[4]

The Second Five-Year Plan

With the Arusha Declaration, a new development strategy was tried. The main features of this approach were later recommended by the distinguished economist W. Arthur Lewis in a published lecture on the establishment of a more equitable international economic order.

> The way to create a new international order is to eliminate . . . low-productivity workers in food by transforming their productivity. This would change the factoral terms of tropical trade and raise the prices of the traditional agricultural exports. It would also create an agricultural surplus that would support industrial production for the home market. These countries would then be less dependent on the rest of the world for finance or for their engine of growth.[5]

Following this logic but still lacking access to politically acceptable investment capital, Tanzania's Second Five-Year Plan (1969–1974) emphasized wealth-generating industry and labor-intensive agriculture. Economic necessity and moral choice were both conveyed in the plan's slogan: *Watu na juhudi yao ndio shina la maendeleo* ("People and their hard work are the foundation of development").

Reflecting the national commitment to socialism and self-reliance, the urban component of the second development plan stressed import substitution and capital-goods production in a largely nationalized industrial sector. Eighty-four percent of all industrial investment was to be made by the government, aiming toward a 7 percent total increase in productivity.

The central element of the second plan was not industry, however, but agriculture. The first plan's emphasis on mechanized cash-crop production was rejected in favor of self-help contributions to increased cash- and food-crop yields. Top priority was given to the creation of *ujamaa* villages in all parts of Tanzania, by "mobilizing the full range of governmental and political institutions behind the principles of *ujamaa*."[6] More than 15 percent of estimated development expenditure was set aside for agriculture, and less than 2 percent was allocated to manufacturing and processing. Infrastructural support accounted for more than 75 percent of projected spending and was focused on villagization and other rural applications.[7]

The second plan embodied three improvements over the first. It incorporated specific regional development programs instead of confining its analysis and goals to the national level. It contained a detailed estimate of specialized skill requirements and training capacities. (Such a study had been completed for the 1964–1969 plan, but had not been published until six months after this plan was begun.) Finally, the second plan pledged itself only to projects that could be

Figure 5.1. A Tanzanian Marketplace.

implemented within two years, leaving the final three years for additions, changes, and deletions within the overall goal framework.[8]

The second plan, slightly less optimistic than the first, set an annual growth rate target of 6.5 percent. In fact, the GDP increased at an average annual rate of only 4.8 percent between 1969 and 1974, with a real per capita gain approaching 1 percent when measured against a population growth rate of 3 percent or more.[9] The rate of return on the government's huge infrastructural investments was slow, and the annual agricultural growth rate was a disappointing 2.7 percent.[10] Between 1969 and 1974 the value of major cash crops increased by nearly 5 percent, but per capita food production fell and the cost of living rose by more than 50 percent.[11] Lackluster performance in Tanzania's most critical economic sector resulted not only from the droughts of 1973 and 1974, but also from an agricultural pricing policy that taxed farmers to subsidize urban consumers and from a villagization program that seriously disrupted crop production.

Industrial output registered a substantial gain of 122 percent during the second plan,[12] but this increase was small in cash terms and depended heavily on foreign raw materials and financial inputs. The plan had failed to develop an industrial strategy compatible with the larger objectives of socialism and self-reliance, and this failure caused the country to become even more deeply enmeshed in unfavorable trade and aid relationships.[13] It also perpetuated the inequality in urban and rural incomes—urban incomes were between five and six times rural ones—which helped further to diminish agricultural incentives. The urban minimum wage was increased by 100 percent in real purchasing power, and by 1974 only about 30 percent of all rural dwellers enjoyed a consuming capacity equal to or greater than that of minimum-wage earners.[14]

The subsistence sector was placed in a particularly desperate predicament by the end of the second plan. The national food supply could not be maintained for two straight years of poor weather without recourse to foreign purchases or aid. Aid dependency increased as agricultural productivity sagged and the trade and balance-of-payments situations worsened. The cost of imports rose from Shs.1.7 billion ($243 million) in 1969 to Shs.5.4 billion ($771 million) in 1974. During the same period, the value of domestic exports increased from Shs.1.8 billion ($257 million) to only Shs.2.9 billion ($414 million). The balance of trade shifted from a positive Shs.83 million ($12 million) in 1969 to a negative Shs.2.5 billion ($357 million) in 1974, combined with a balance-of-payments deficit of nearly Shs.2 billion ($286 million).[15]

In spite of considerable success in reducing basic poverty and improving the quality of life for most Tanzanians, the advance toward socialism and self-reliance was seriously endangered on the economic front. The Third Five Year Plan (1976–1981) sought to solve this problem by discouraging foreign economic inputs, aiming toward self-sufficiency in food and other products, and insisting on increased productivity through more efficient work organization and stricter discipline.

The Third Five Year Plan

Tanzania's most recent development plan did not become operational until late 1976. An "interim strategy" was pursued from mid-1974 to enable the country to recover from the losses of preceding years. The immediate goals were price and wage stability, a reduction in the balance-of-payments deficit to an acceptable Shs.1.25 billion ($156 million),[16] and a 5 to 6 percent annual economic growth rate. In 1975 the GDP increased by 4.6 percent, and in 1976, by 5.2 percent. Prices and wages were stabilized, but at a cost of negative employment growth and financial hardship for salaried employees. Much of the balance-of-payments problem resulted from large food imports made necessary by villagization and by the 1973 and 1974 droughts. Food supplies increased by 8 percent in 1975 and again in 1976, but the production and export of other commodities was not enough to prevent large trade and balance-of-payments deficits for these years.[17] Tanzania continued to rely on foreign financial assistance to help clear its debts, mainly in the form of credits from the International Monetary Fund. The economic outlook was somewhat brighter on Zanzibar, where the Jumbe government released about Shs.500 million ($62 million) in clove profits to cover recurrent expenditures and finance development projects.[18]

In his 1977 progress report on the Arusha Declaration, President Nyerere expressed satisfaction with the social-welfare achievements of the Second Five-Year Plan and interim strategy. He had reason to be content. Primary school enrollments had risen from 825,000 in 1967 to 1,532,000 in 1975. Nearly 2 million men and women had passed a literacy test in August 1975, having participated in a nationwide program to reduce adult illiteracy. Similar educational campaigns had been conducted to promote local sanitation and health, and the number of rural health centers had grown from 42 in 1967 to 152 by 1976. During this same period, 610 maternal and child care centers had been opened and rural medical staffing had increased by more than 200 percent. Approximately Shs.500 million had been spent on upgrading local water supplies.[19]

Inequality had also been lessened under the second plan. As noted in Chapter 4, by 1976 the ratio of the top government salary to the minimum wage was reduced to about fifteen to one, far below the seventy-to-one ratio that Tanganyika inherited with independence. Rural cooperative societies had been formally abolished in 1976 and their managerial functions assumed by village councils that better conveyed the needs of less successful agricultural producers.

Nyerere was less sanguine about the economy's productive sectors and argued for more emphasis on working efficiency, self-help labor contributions, and profitability in the nationalized government corporations. These recommendations were discussed and endorsed by the party and incorporated into the 1976–1981 development plan.

The Third Five Year Plan projected a total public-sector investment of slightly more than Shs.30 billion ($3.75 billion). On an annual basis this sum approximated that of the 1977-1978 operating budget and seemed appropriate to the 6 percent annual economic growth rate anticipated under the plan. The actual growth in GDP averaged an encouraging 5.9 percent between 1977 and 1978.[20] On the other hand, future investments were calculated in constant prices, and inflation made it unlikely that this growth rate could be sustained. The prospect of attaining the 6 percent goal was rendered even more doubtful by an expectation that nearly half of all investment capital would come from foreign sources.

The objectives of the third plan are conservative by previous standards and were aimed at consolidating the rural revolution and moving the country closer to national self-reliance. Productive goals included food self-sufficiency by 1981 and the more efficient use of natural resources, the latter to be achieved by concentrating on agricultural processing and by exploiting local fuels and minerals in support of industrial activities. Emphasis was placed on industrial projects that were likely to make early returns on their investments. The plan also focused on economic infrastructure, prescribing improvements in scientific and technical education, the satisfaction of industrial requirements for water and electricity, and the expansion of transportation, communication, and storage facilities. Social infrastructure was to be further developed by completing the universal primary education program, by providing increased water supplies and basic medical services to the urban and rural areas, and by improving village housing and development planning.

The plan made clear that the new objectives could not be reached simply by throwing money at them but would also require tighter work organization and sterner discipline.

> Tanzania will be built through our own efforts by intelligently using our talents. It is therefore imperative that every Tanzanian work harder and more diligently than ever before. Measures will be taken to ensure that the Party has effective control over all

implementing institutions and that the people are involved in all economic activities by using new methods and modern technology.[21]

Although the period covered by the third development plan had only just ended at the time of writing, a preliminary assessment can be made of the plan in operation and the directions in which it has moved Tanzania.

THE ECONOMICS OF CHOICE

President Nyerere has often reminded Tanzanians that planning and development involve choosing among competing alternatives; and the deeper the poverty of a nation, the more difficult the choices. Table 5.1 suggests that, in the aggregate, current development policies have at least temporarily avoided the hardest choices. With its balanced commitments to developmental and social-welfare investments and to the mainland's less and more well-watered regions, the Third Five-Year Plan displayed little sectoral or geographical bias favoring either economic growth or socioeconomic equality. Nyerere has also observed that failing to choose is itself a choice. In attempting to realize their larger social and economic goals, political and governmental leaders must try to avoid the unfortunate but dangerously possible outcomes of equality without growth or growth without equality.

Growth Through Incentives

Tanzania entered the 1978-1979 fiscal year with a balanced budget, but one that was highly contingent on the availability of foreign funds. The budget included local receipts of Shs.7.5 billion ($937.5 million), Shs.3.2 billion ($400 million) in foreign loans and investments, and international assistance grants of Shs.1.5 billion ($187.5 million). These resources were intended to help reverse the negative economic trends of the preceding ten years.

The prognosis was not good. The annual rate of inflation had increased from 1.8 percent in 1967 to 12.3 percent by 1978. Per capita food production dropped by a total of 7 percent during the decade of villagization, although total agricultural outut improved at an average annual rate of more than 4 percent. Population growth climbed to an average annual rate of more than 3 percent, and the per capita food intake satisfied only 89 percent of daily caloric requirements. Industrial production rose by less than 1 percent, while directly nonremunerative social services more than doubled. Although private consumption increased at an average annual rate of nearly 6 percent between 1970 and 1978, investment growth averaged only 1.9 percent—down from the 9.8 percent attained in the decade from 1960.[22]

Tanzania's international economic position appeared scarcely less precarious than its domestic economic position in 1978. The balance-of-payments deficit soared to Shs.3.5 billion ($437.5 million), and the external debt had mushroomed from 19.4 to 25.1 percent of GDP in the preceding seven years. Less than one month's supply of foreign exchange remained on hand at any given time to cover necessary imports.[23]

Table 5.1

Third Five Year Plan Regional Allocations of Development Funds
(Percent of Allocations)[a]

Region	Productive Sectors	Economic Infrastructure	Social Infrastructure	Share of Total Regional Allocations
		Least Well-Watered		
Mtwara	26	17	57	4.8
Rukwa	20	30	40	4.5
Shinyanga	30	20	50	4.5
Tabora	30	30	40	5.5
Lindi	30	20	50	4.6
		Marginally Well-Watered		
Dodoma	30	18	52	4.9
Singida	31	22	47	4.6
Arusha	47	12	41	5.8
		Moderately Well-Watered		
Mwanza	28	23	49	4.9
Iringa	29	37	33	4.8
Mbeya	30	20	50	5.1
Tanga	39	20	40	5.0
Morogoro	30	30	40	5.3
Dar es Salaam	8	37	55	4.8
Mara	30	20	50	5.0
Kigoma	32	18	48	5.2
Ruvuma	30	30	40	4.2
Coast	21	32	47	5.3
		Most Well-Watered		
Kilimanjaro	30	23	47	5.3
West Lake	30	20	50	5.0

Source: Tanzania, Third Five Year Plan for Economic and Social Development,
1st July, 1976 - 30th June, 1981, Volume 1, Part 2, Regional Perspectives
(Dar es Salaam: National Printing Co., Ltd., n.d.), p. 127. Like its earlier
counterparts, the Third Five Year Plan covered only the twenty mainland regions.
The five Zanzibari regions have continued to operate under their own development
plans.

[a]Some percentages do not equal 100 because of minor errors and rounding.

In his review of events since the Arusha Declaration, President Nyerere emphasized the need to perfect the economic innovations already in place before em-
barking on further advances toward socialism and self-reliance. Because of the
economic stagnation that stubbornly persisted after 1977, private incentives were
reintroduced after an eleven-year lapse. This unplanned policy choice raises two
fundamental questions: whether the inducements provided to stimulate growth
will be sufficient to accomplish the task, and whether they will require a permanent dependence on foreign economic assistance, helping to create an internationally subsidized class system instead of a self-reliant and egalitarian society.
These questions remain unanswered.

The development strategy was still committed in the early 1980s to self-sufficiency in food and other basic resources and to a postponement of rewards that require an extensive urban industrial sector. In a departure from the Third Five Year Plan, the strategy included such inducements as more consumer goods, higher farm prices, some lower taxes, and increased private investment opportunities. The incentive campaign was interrupted by external events, and particularly by the costly war with Uganda. Despite these diversions, or perhaps partly because of them, the party-government has made one noteworthy improvement in its otherwise indeterminate attempts to improve economic performance. A kind of ideologically disciplined pragmatism has found its way into the Tanzanian policy process. This attitude permits the unceremonious replacement of policies that do not work with those that might, even if the modification necessitates a temporary return to options once rejected on ideological grounds. The present emphasis on incentives provides one example of this new flexibility. Another is the latest changes in the rural cooperative movement.

The cooperative societies were abolished in 1976 because they were judged to be administratively top-heavy, corrupt, and biased in favor of the more prosperous cash-crop farmers. In an effort to make local cooperative activities more compatible with Nyerere's socialist objectives, the societies' organizational and social functions were turned over to village councils recently established under the Villages and *Ujamaa* Villages Act. Wholesale marketing, storage, and processing services were transferred to government-controlled purchasing authorities and the National Milling Corporation. The villages were thus placed in charge of overseeing most of Tanzania's food-crop production and much of its cash-crop output. The village councils demonstrated their inability to bear this heavy administrative burden and to deal effectively with the national marketing and processing agencies, which have experienced their own efficiency problems. Without fanfare or apology, the decision was made in 1981 to reinstate the cooperative movement. This is considered an interim step made necessary by the temporary inability of the villages to perform these tasks. The ultimate goal seems still to return these responsibilities to the village councils.

In the meantime, Tanzania has continued to experience severe economic difficulties in the rural and urban areas. Cash-crop production declined by a commodity average of 22 percent between 1977 and 1978. In contrast, good harvests and rising producer prices resulted in local food surpluses during the same years. National food supplies also increased, and by 1979 marketing difficulties and a lack of storage facilities had forced the government to export more than 200,000 tons of grain. The drought of 1980 quickly transformed an embarrassing surplus into a perilous shortage, and the drought continued into 1981. Low export earnings and the likelihood of large-scale food imports spelled economic trouble as Tanzania entered its third decade of independence.

In the industrial sector, manufacturing output is now three times greater than in 1967, and some consumer goods are more available than in past years. Private investment has benefited from the relaxation of import controls over manufacturing inputs and has helped to fill the gap between family enterprises and the nationalized government corporations. Small industries are developing in such vital areas as cement and spare parts.

The situation of urban workers is less encouraging. They have received less than a 10 percent increase in wages since 1975, and consumer prices have risen by more than 20 percent. The pressure has been eased by tax reforms, which have transferred some of the financial burden from employees with large families to consumers of luxury items, such as beer, cigarettes, and liquor. This relief has not provided sufficient economic incentive to increase labor support for the Third Five Year Plan. Workers' councils were established between 1969 and 1971 to encourage employee participation in management and also to enhance production levels. The councils are still in operation under the direction of the renamed Union of Tanzanian Workers (NUTA), which is affiliated with the CCM and shares the government's productionist viewpoint on industrial relations. But the councils themselves tend to focus on distributive benefits, such as shorter working hours, overtime pay, improved living conditions, and higher-quality meals in shop canteens.[24]

In 1977 President Nyerere lamented the sorry state of industrial discipline and the party's sheltering of unproductive workers. He complained that "in many places TANU and NUTA branches are still better able at protecting workers . . . from [the rightful consequences of] bad workmanship or slackness" than at encouraging increased output.[25] Productivity has not improved since 1977, and reported cases of managerial corruption are becoming more numerous. In January 1981 the minister for communications and transport and the chairman and managing director of Air Tanzania Corporation were dismissed for improprieties in the allocation of contracts. In the same month, a multimillion-shilling scandal was uncovered, involving unauthorized car rentals by government ministries and corporations.[26]

On the international economic scene, the country is trying to lower its huge trade and balance-of-payments deficits by developing its own fuels, fertilizers, and industrial raw materials. Exploration is now under way to determine whether nickel, iron, coal, and other minerals can be economically exploited. A U.S. firm is helping to build a fertilizer plant, which will use locally available natural gas. But even if the explorations are successful, commercial mineral extraction will be expensive and cannot begin before the late 1980s, and the fertilizer factory will not be completed until 1985.[27] Negative balances of trade and payments are perpetuated by the high price of petrochemical imports, by increasingly frequent food shortages, and by Tanzania's regional trade difficulties in eastern Africa (see Chapter 6). Profitability seems as elusive in the regional as in the national economic sphere.

Growth Versus Equality

The party-government has placed itself in firm control of the "commanding heights" of industrial production, has rationalized the pattern of rural settlement in a manner more conducive to efficient agriculture, and has taken important strides toward building an educated and healthy work force. The organizational and social framework for development is largely established, but it has not yet resulted in economic growth. According to the basic tenets of the Arusha Declaration and the goals of the Third Five Year Plan, growth must not only be realized, but be brought about in a way that will ensure social and economic equality. It may be that growth and equality are mutually exclusive objectives in contemporary Tanzania. Vice-President Jumbe has called for more private industries[28] but has not suggested how to prevent a further widening of the ratio between urban and rural incomes and the consolidation of the incipient class division between the cities and the countryside. Members of parliament request additional agricultural inputs and higher farm prices,[29] but they do not consider the social and political effects of economic rewards that must inevitably benefit the richer more than the poorer rural areas. No one is prepared to say when the villages will be able to raise their productivity and at the same time handle their own affairs efficiently and equitably. The original village settlement program demonstrated that centrally funded rural transformation can quickly lead to large income differences between assisted and unassisted localities and to an escalating demand for unearned amenities.

The party-government is also seeking national self-sufficiency so that it can obtain the necessary economic freedom to guarantee increasing benefits for all Tanzanians. If it can be achieved, autarchy will provide the policymaking elites with plenty of autonomy to make whatever distributive decisions they desire. But the establishment of economic independence will require a long period of capital investment, significant export earnings to pay for this investment, and at least a temporary reduction in the growth of welfare benefits. The leadership must also quickly lower the foreign exchange deficit and lessen the country's dependence on foreign budgetary contributions. In 1979 Tanzania looked to the International Monetary Fund (IMF) for help in confronting the last two of these imperatives. An IMF team was dispatched to Dar es Salaam, but it could not reach agreement with the Tanzanian authorities on the financial and monetary terms of the proposed assistance. In particular, the IMF insisted that Tanzania devalue its currency; freeze certain wages; alter its import, credit, and retail pricing policies; implement selective personnel changes; and curtail health and educational expenditures in favor of larger investments in export crops. President Nyerere replaced his finance minister for supporting the IMF plan. He also accused the IMF of trying to intervene in Tanzania's internal affairs and of acting on behalf of industrial countries that were hoping to confine Tanzania to its colonial role as an exporter of primary products. These protestations were futile. Tanzania had already been compelled to devalue its currency before the IMF visit and had required $152 million in IMF credits and loans between 1974 and 1978. The government was now forced to agree on the major conditions of a further assistance package, which extended some $222 million in credits until 1983. The agreement was suspended after only one drawing of funds because Tanzania was unable to satisfy its terms. Negotiations on a revised agreement, involving about $475 million, broke down during July 1981.

The prospects are not promising for an early transition to self-reliant socialism. Tanzanian workers and farmers expect a much improved standard of living, which cannot be sustained through a continued reliance on bilateral and multilateral largesse. Conversely, attempts to gain economic independence run the risk of turning Tanzanian policymakers toward an overwhelming preoccupation with the creation of wealth and foreign exchange earnings and away from their public commitment to equality and social welfare. The question must be faced of what is more important, a growing and increasingly self-reliant economy fueled by unequally distributed incentives and remunerations or an economically stagnant but egalitarian society dedicated to the advancement of even its least productive members.

In 1972 one scholar argued that Tanzania was putting the international system to work in support of socialism and self-reliance by controlling the sources and flow of aid "in such a way as to minimize the disruption which might be caused by the failure of foreign sources of finance to materialize."[30] Until the economic catastrophes of the 1970s, this take-it-or-leave-it attitude toward foreign assistance was made possible by the Arusha Declaration's rejection of money as the principal engine of development and by the declaration's insistence on rural modernization through self-help. Of dire economic necessity, export promotion has again come to be viewed as a key element in Tanzanian development, and it will require the same high levels of financial investment that the declaration opposed. The internationally funded share of new development projects grew from about 49 percent in 1972 to nearly 70 percent in 1981.

By returning to the economic policy orientations of the 1960s, the party-government may be tempted once more to place growth above equality. The inequalities of development constitute a permanent ideological challenge for Tanzania; yet the immediate practical problem is not socioeconomic class formation, but economic survival itself. The International Labour Office has acknowledged that in the near term, the country must be prepared to settle for economic growth primarily through the modernization of small-farm agriculture.[31] Making the villages more productive may eventually reduce Tanzania's international dependency and retard the growth of a domestic class system. If the rate of rural development remains at the level of the early 1980s, agricultural productivity increases will not keep pace with population growth and urbanization, nor will they generate enough food or surplus capital to alleviate the country's frequent environmental emergencies. As the 1980s began, insufficient attention was being paid to agricultural incentives or to the farmers' practical knowledge. Locally assigned party-government officials tended openly to display their formal training and authority, which were often inappropriate to specific ecological conditions, material needs, and pragmatic interests. Marketing, storage, and transportation services remained sporadic and inefficient. Producers' prices for food crops were still tightly controlled in order to provide relatively inexpensive food for the inflation-prone cities. In an effort to increase foreign exchange earnings, cash-crop prices were frequently set below international levels.

If the party-government cannot even guarantee an adequate food supply, it cannot begin to fulfill the rising material aspirations of its constituents. The elites are painfully aware that the rural and urban masses have their own ways of responding to both kinds of economic failure.

THE ECONOMICS OF SURVIVAL

A decade after independence, President Nyerere reaffirmed his faith in grassroots participation as both a tool and a goal of development.

> As far as we are concerned, the people's freedom to determine their own priorities, to organize themselves, and their own advance in welfare, is an important part of our objective. It cannot be postponed to some future time. The people's active and continued voluntary participation in the struggle is an important part of our objective because only through this participation will the people develop. And to us, the development of the nation means the development of people.[32]

What Nyerere had in mind, of course, was self-sacrificing participation in support of the party, the government, and the national objectives of socialism and self-reliance. This kind of involvement has substantially been achieved at the leadership level and has slowed if not completely halted the evolution of a political elite class. Anyone who has recently dealt with Tanzanian political and governmental officials can agree that "the food they eat, the houses they live in, their holiday travelling, their forms of entertainment, their plans for retirement, all indicate that they have remained intimately part of the Tanzanian scene."[33]

Nonetheless, the urban and rural masses are discontented with the conditions under which they must live. In spite of the regime's best efforts to enhance the quality of Tanzanian life, the economic plight of the people remains serious. In some localities life itself is endangered by chronic food shortages. Faced with uncertainties of this magnitude, increasing numbers of Tanzanians have participated by reducing their support for the regime. This response to adversity is understandable, but it presents the party-government with a tragic dilemma. The regime can curtail voluntary expressions of interest and subject the country to the disciplines of a vanguard elite, or it can try to satisfy those demands that, for economic and perhaps political reasons, appear to be the most critical. Choosing the first alternative would mean abandoning the commitment to an open and democratic political process. Selecting the second would quickly end any hope of completing the transition to socialism and equality. Mainly because of Nyerere's personal influence, the national leadership has opted for neither of these alternatives, and an uneasy atmosphere of irresolution surrounds the Tanzanian policy process. Decisions cannot be delayed for long: President Nyerere has announced his intention to retire from active government service by 1985, and the citizenry, through its actions, is already beginning to reject many of the sacrifices required by Nyerere's formula for socialism and self-reliance. The people no less than the leadership are concerned with development and, if this is not possible, with survival.

Survival in the Cities

The party-government has tried to increase industrial productivity by encouraging worker participation in management. The workers' councils have not functioned well in this role, proving themselves more effective as grievance committees. Industrial inefficiency persists and productivity remains low. Employment is also a problem. The percentage of the labor force in industry increased from 4 percent in 1960 to approximately 6 percent in 1979, but the average annual rate of urbanization grew from about 6 percent during the 1960s to nearly 10 percent in the 1970s and early 1980s. These trends run counter to the primary emphasis on agricultural and rural development and threaten to turn the urban areas into densely populated islands of human misery and political alienation. Yet the greatest dangers of economic distress and political withdrawal lie not in the towns but rather in the countryside.

Survival in the Villages

Serious students of Tanzanian local affairs are reaching agreement that the rapidly growing rural population holds the country's fate in its hands, but it is withdrawing from further cooperation in national economic and political life. "The present agricultural picture is one of a peaceful revolt, an unwillingness to produce, or to become part of the wider system. There has been a turning back to the small farm/small plot for survival-level farming. Production incentives do not exist, nor has the government been able to coerce the farmers into greater productivity."[34]

The farmers have reason to opt out of the system. The villagization program was not followed by effective measures to restore food production in the poorest regions. The decentralization of administration reinforced poverty in these regions by facilitating the informal establishment of self-serving fiefdoms in the more prosperous rural areas. Even here commercial producers have suffered from insufficient technical advice; from inadequate marketing, storage, and transport services; and from what they see as artificially depressed crop prices. They have also witnessed scandal and corruption in the cooperative movement and have themselves increasingly turned to smuggling and black marketing. For their part, subsistence farmers have simply exercised their "exit option"[35] and retreated from meaningful involvement in the economy. Today this factor may be as responsible for Tanzania's impending famines as are its poor weather conditions and negative terms of trade.

The marginality of rural society has served as an asset, enabling it to weather two exploitative colonial regimes and a well-meaning but developmentally inept nationalist government: "Tanzanians have great ability to survive, to be resilient, to cut back and carry on under the most adverse conditions. That they have had to do this periodically is an important fact that underlines the national picture. Political stability has in fact been maintained in part because this peasantry has such flexibility and resilience."[36] This has been true in the past, but the specter of mass hunger now rises over Tanzania,[37] and the country's destiny will be determined by how well the political and governmental authorities can recapture the support of a skeptical and increasingly desperate rural society.

6

International Leadership and Dependence

Tanzania's party-government has achieved widespread, if politically superficial, consensus on its foreign policies. Here, as in domestic affairs, the record is one of numerous moral triumphs but few practical victories. Tanzania has consistently championed political and economic unity in eastern Africa, but the country has become involved in a succession of economic, political, and even military confrontations with several of its neighbors. Nyerere has long served as Africa's most articulate proponent of national self-reliance and the creation of a more equitable international economic order, yet no other African country is less self-sufficient and economically more dependent than Tanzania. Nevertheless, international issues have exercised a unifying influence on the society, particularly issues linking Tanzania with the political liberation of southern Africa. Tanzanians are justly proud of their government's uncompromising opposition to the last vestiges of colonialism and racism in Africa. Their satisfaction has not yet been negated by the material sacrifices they have been required to make on behalf of the southern African liberation movements.

Nyerere, Tanzania, and the World

Tanzania's foreign policy has an uncommonly moralistic quality. As in the domestic arena, this philosophical orientation is based on the thought of Julius Nyerere. He has frequently been compelled to adjust his design for a just and democratic society in Tanzania to the harsh realities of his place and time. Nyerere has compromised his values only grudgingly and, interestingly enough, less in foreign than in domestic policy. Applied internationally, his conceptions of equality, democracy, and socialism have imparted a degree of moral rigidity to an area of politics usually distinguished by its amoral pragmatism.

Since independence, Tanzanian diplomacy has focused on three major goals: the attainment of independence and majority rule throughout Africa, the maintenance of an active but nonaligned relationship with each of the major power blocs, and the encouragement of equal economic and political cooperation with other developing countries. These objectives are not unique in the Third World. Less typical is Nyerere's single-minded determination to pursue them, if necessary at the expense of Tanzania's immediate political and economic interests.

Nyerere's goals for an acceptable international order are idealistic, but his evaluation of the obstacles preventing their realization is starkly realistic. Chief among these impediments is the pervasive evil of racism.

> The principles of freedom and equality have no validity unles they are of universal validity; and the principle of racial supremacy is invalid unless it is universally valid. Conflict between these two conceptions of humanity is inevitable. Where they meet, the conflict will become an active one. Tanzania's concern with the situation in Southern Africa is thus not something which is extraneous to our other policies. It is a matter affecting our security. It is central to everything we do.[1]

Next to racial subjugation, in Nyerere's view, the greatest enemies of peace and human dignity are wealthy countries representing both capitalist and socialist ideologies. These systems maintain their favored positions by keeping the majority of the world's population in a condition of poverty and indentured servitude. In order to hold their own against these rich and powerful nations, poor countries must do more than simply denounce them.

> It is no longer enough for non-aligned states to meet and complain to each other and to the world about international bullying. Everyone now knows that this international bullying goes on. And we have already declared our intention of standing up to such behaviour, and of refusing to become permanent allies of any big and bullying power. Also, we have declared our opposition to colonialism until it has become a series of hackneyed clichés.[2]

Nyerere recognized that the vulnerability of the poor will be overcome not by the sudden enlightenment of the rich, but rather by the willingness of the poor to unite and to share their meager resources. Addressing a meeting of nonaligned nations in 1970, he admonished:

> When we really consider the modern world, and its divisions between the haves and the have-nots, not one member of this Conference is anything but a pauper. And like paupers, we shall really win a decent and secure livelihood, and maintain our dignity and independence, only if we act together. . . . Will we recognize our economic and political need for each other? If we do this, the less poor among us have to act in a manner which eases the development of the more poor, and thus allows us all to maintain a solid and united front. And the more poor have to acknowledge that these others cannot stand still in their development, but that we have to co-operate for mutual benefit, with give and take on both sides.[3]

The world view espoused by Julius Nyerere is that of an idealist whose many disappointments have not yet dampened his will to prevail against formidable odds. This description also fits most of Tanzanian foreign policy.

SOUTHERN AFRICA

Nyerere has made Tanzania the leading "front-line" African state in the struggle against colonialism and racial discrimination in southern Africa. In close cooperation with Zambia, Tanzania has provided sanctuary and material support for liberation movements of Mozambique, Rhodesia (now Zimbabwe), South-West Africa (Namibia), and the Republic of South Africa itself. At great cost to themselves, Tanzanians have consistently refused to compromise on the principles of self-government and majority rule for all Africans.

The Early Years

Between 1961 and 1965, the Tanzanian government received thousands of political refugees from southern Africa and permitted them to organize for their independence struggles at home. These groups included the Front for the Liberation of Mozambique, the African National Congress and Pan-African Congress from South Africa, the Zimbabwe African People's Union of Rhodesia, and the South-West African People's Organization. President Nyerere also helped to establish the Organization of African Unity (OAU) in 1963[4] and offered Dar es Salaam as headquarters for its African Liberation Committee.

Having failed to obtain Western support for the liberation movements he was hosting, Nyerere allowed them to receive arms and training from socialist states, including the Soviet Union, the People's Republic of China, and Algeria. Nyerere was saddened by the violent tendency of anticolonial conflicts in the south, which differed so much from Tanzania's own transition to independence. He was also concerned that support for the liberation movements came entirely from the Eastern bloc, whose internal disagreements did not prevent the movements and their Tanzanian patron from being involved in cold war competition. In spite of these misgivings, Nyerere was willing to risk Eastern intervention and Western hostility in the interests of southern African independence. He soon paid the price of this choice. For over ten years after 1965, Tanzania suffered interruptions in friendly relations with its largest foreign aid donors, Britain and the United States, partly as a result of its policies on southern Africa.

The Arusha Declaration and the 1971 TANU guidelines (the *Mwongozo*) reasserted Tanzanian leadership in Africa's final assault on colonialism and racism. The declaration pledged the country "to co-operate with all political parties in Africa engaged in the liberation of all Africa." The *Mwongozo* emphasized the essentially conflictual nature of this effort. The guidelines castigated Western countries for not responding to the African plea for freedom and rejected a continuation of diplomatic attempts to secure this assistance. The *Mwongozo* committed the party and government to increased logistical and political support for full-scale guerrilla campaigns against the Portuguese, Rhodesian, and South African regimes south of the Ruvuma and Zambezi rivers. These exhortations were translated into a series of strategies that still guide Tanzania in its southern African policy.

Progress in the Continuing Struggle

Five major components of the contemporary Tanzanian approach to southern African liberation have been identified:[5]

1. Continued moral and material support for the military and paramilitary liberation movements.

2. Diplomatic recognition of these movements, in the hope of increasing their international respectability.
3. Reconciliation of internal differences within and among the liberation groups, to increase their effectiveness and reduce the likelihood of postindependence political violence in their countries.
4. Diplomatic and propaganda pressures aimed at isolating the minority regimes in southern Africa, combined with an effort to promote the enforcement and extension of international sanctions against these regimes.
5. Provision of opportunities for close communication among the liberation movements, and between them and similar organizations in other parts of the world, to strengthen their members' resolve and solidarity.

Vigorous implementation of these strategies helped to alienate Tanzania from more pragmatic African states, notably Malawi, which chose a path of peaceful coexistence with the minority governments. Tanzania also annoyed the United States, which was locked into its NATO military alliance with Portugal and seemed determined to protect its lucrative business interests in Rhodesia, Angola, and South Africa.[6] Ignoring these regional and international complications, Tanzania played an important role in the eventual decolonization of Mozambique, Angola, and Zimbabwe. In the early 1980s it continued to provide leadership in Namibia's halting movement toward independence.

President Nyerere has consistently preferred negotiated settlements to armed conflicts in southern Africa. Nevertheless, he strongly supported the Mozambican war of liberation against the recalcitrant Portuguese and in 1976 sent Tanzanian troops to help protect the newly independent country from Rhodesian military incursions.[7] Soon after these troops arrived, Nyerere warned Rhodesia that "Tanzanian troops will be used if the independence of Mozambique, Zambia and other Front-Line States is threatened—and we mean what we say."[8] As chairman of an informal organization that had come to be known as the Front-Line African States (now comprising Tanzania, Zambia, Botswana, Mozambique, and Angola), Nyerere called a meeting of his fellow presidents in January 1977. At this meeting a mutual defense agreement was reached, according to which an attack on any one of the member countries would be regarded as an attack on them all.

Subsequently, the Tanzanian role in southern Africa shifted from a concentration on military support to an emphasis on discussion and mediation. Tanzanian diplomacy helped to bring together the various parties with interests in the Rhodesian conflict[9] into a series of heated negotiations and reluctant compromises that led to Zimbabwean independence in April 1980. Concerning Namibia, Tanzania has supplied logistical support to the South-West African People's Organization (SWAPO) and has consistently chided the international community for not eliminating South African control over the country. Nyerere applauded the recent efforts of Western powers to bring about a peaceful Namibian settlement, but he has become impatient with their lack of results. At a January 1981 meeting of the Organization of African Unity, he encouraged greater military support for SWAPO unless the current round of negotiations was successful in creating an independent and fully representative Namibia.

The crusade for southern African liberation continues; and Tanzania remains pledged to advance the struggle until all countries in the region, including South Africa, have achieved independence and majority rule. This commitment has not been reduced by the society's economic crises or even by its increasing dependence on food imports from countries Tanzania considers supportive of South Africa. In order to prevail, one must first be able to eat.

EASTERN AND CENTRAL AFRICA

The search for interterritorial unity forms one of the most persistent themes in the history of twentieth-century eastern Africa. This quest was begun by the British in the early 1900s and was given fresh impetus when Germany was expelled from eastern Africa during World War I. By the 1920s and early 1930s, important steps had been taken toward the economic integration of Tanganyika, Kenya, and Uganda. Because these and subsequent initiatives have so heavily influenced Tanzania's contemporary relations with its neighboring states, they warrant a brief review.[10]

The Movement Toward Regional Integration

One of the more positive legacies of British colonial rule was its partial economic unification of Tanganyika, Kenya, and Uganda. The governors of the three territories met regularly during the early 1920s to discuss the requirements of shared economic development. By 1927 British eastern Africa was joined in a system of common tariffs, duty-free transfers of imported goods, a single currency, and integrated services in such vital areas as railroads, customs, posts and telegraphs, and defense. A regional income tax was introduced in 1939. The East African High Commission (EAHC) was established in 1948 to coordinate and extend the ad hoc arrangements of previous years. The EAHC included a Central Legislative Assembly that was empowered to appropriate funds for a wide range of regional activities, including customs and excise collections, railways and harbors administration, civil aviation, postal and electronic communications, and Makerere College. (Makerere, located in Kampala, Uganda, was the region's only degree-granting educational institution until the early 1960s.) In recognition of the swift decolonization of eastern Africa, the EAHC was replaced in 1961 by the East African Common Services Organization (EACSO). This action localized interterritorial cooperation by transferring its oversight from the British government to the chief ministers of Tanganyika, Kenya, and Uganda.

Integrative progress was not confined to economics and education. A regional political organization had emerged during the late 1950s, although not at the behest of the British. In 1958 the Pan-African Freedom Movement for East and Central Africa (PAFMECA) was formed at Mwanza by African political leaders representing the nationalist movements of Tanganyika, Kenya, Uganda, Zanzibar, Nyasaland (now Malawi), Northern Rhodesia (now Zambia), and Southern Rhodesia (now Zimbabwe). Membership was expanded in 1959 and again in 1962, when the organization was renamed the Pan-African Freedom Movement for East, Central, and Southern Africa (PAFMECSA). It was administered by a permanent secretariat in Dar es Salaam.

PAFMECSA's immediate objective was to present a united front in support
of rapid and nonviolent transition to independence in all of eastern, central, and
southern Africa. A more tentative secondary goal was the progressive political
unification of its member states. This process was intended to begin with the creation of an East African federation, once Kenya, Uganda, and Zanzibar had joined
Tanganyika in gaining independence. It was soon discovered, however, that the
advance toward independence depended more on internal than on international
pressures and that interterritorial political unity would be more difficult to attain
than had previously been anticipated. PAFMECSA was disbanded in 1963 after
the Organization of African Unity was formed to promote a more limited conception of pan-Africanism that was compatible with the preservation of national
sovereignty.[11]

Although he welcomed the OAU, Julius Nyerere remained one of Africa's
most ardent supporters of supranational economic and political integration. He
even went so far as to suggest that Tanganyika postpone its own independence
until Zanzibar, Kenya, and Uganda were able to join it in a federation of states.[12]
These countries became independent in 1962 and 1963, and Nyerere immediately
found that neither political unification nor even extensive economic cooperation
would be easily achieved. Because of the nationalist rather than pan-African
orientations of their parties and governments, the political leaders of eastern
Africa decided for the time being to limit their joint endeavors to the economic
sphere. Here too the obstacles were formidable. Since the early colonial period,
Kenya's economic performance had consistently outstripped that of Uganda and
Tanganyika. The distribution of revenues and trade profits under EAHC and
EACSO had reinforced this trend and now threatened to institutionalize an increasingly unbalanced economic relationship between Kenya and its less affluent
partners.

In order to help equalize future development in the three countries, their
respective finance and commerce ministers met at Kampala in 1964 and drafted an
agreement that would have allocated five of eight "interterritorially connected" industries to Tanzania, two to Uganda, and one to Kenya.[13] Kenya refused to ratify
this agreement, evidently fearing the precedent it might set for still other attempts
to retard Kenyan economic growth. In the meantime, Nairobi continued to serve
as the undisputed hub of eastern African industrial and commercial activity. Tanzania responded by imposing a consumption tax on Kenyan imports and a national development tax outside the control of EACSO's East African Income Tax
Department. These measures were followed by the establishment of a separate currency and banking system and by the restriction of selected imports from Kenya
and Uganda. Another modus operandi was clearly needed to prevent the total
collapse of common economic services and preferred trade relations.

In 1967 the three governments concluded the Treaty for East African Co-
Operation, which provided for an East African Community (EAC) and an East
African Common Market (EACM). In particular, the treaty prescribed a common
external tariff and the abolition of all but a few specifically authorized internal
tariffs. The exceptions were temporary customs duties, termed "transfer taxes,"
that could be levied on exports from richer to poorer member states. An East

African Development Bank was also established and instructed to make 80 percent of its investments in Tanzania and Uganda. These and other provisions to ensure equal representation and a fair distribution of the benefits created by the community failed to slow the rate of Kenyan economic ascendancy over Uganda and especially over Tanzania. Kenya's growing economic dominance led to increasing political tensions within the community, which were worsened by the Ugandan coup d'état of January 1971.

National Interests and Regional Conflicts

For Tanzania and eastern Africa as a whole, the 1970s were a period of unprecedented conflict and uncertainty, and the 1980s can only be foreseen as another "decade of doubt."[14]

Tanzania and Uganda. Because of the personal friendship and ideological affinities of Presidents Julius Nyerere and Milton Obote, Tanzania played an indirect role in Obote's downfall. On the basis of his Common Man's Charter, Obote seemed intent on introducing a Tanzanian type of one-party democracy into his communally competitive society. This "move to the left" was strongly opposed by the powerful Baganda society of southern Uganda, which showed its displeasure by backing General Idi Amin in his coup of January 25, 1971. Obote was abroad at the time, and Nyerere offered him asylum, together with about sixteen hundred political supporters and loyalist Ugandan soldiers. Nyerere publicly condemned Amin as a "murderer" and twenty months later authorized Ugandan exiles to attack Uganda in an attempt to oust Amin and reinstate Obote. The countercoup failed, and on October 25, 1972, Tanzania agreed to a cease fire with the Amin regime.

The Tanzanian leadership remained hostile to Amin but endured his periodic threats and refrained from intervening as he proceeded to destroy Uganda's once-viable agricultural economy and to launch a reign of terror that had no precedent in the modern history of eastern Africa. This uneasy peace lasted until October 1978, when Ugandan troops invaded Tanzania and occupied the Kagera Salient, an area of 1,846 square kilometers (710 square miles) in northern West Lake Region. The invaders killed an undetermined number of Tanzanian peasants, carried several hundred schoolgirls across the border to serve as concubines, and destroyed whatever crops and property they could not steal. Amin maintained that the raid was in retribution for an earlier Tanzanian incursion into Uganda. In fact, 200 Ugandan soldiers had mutinied at the military base of Mbarara, had fled into Tanzania, and had been pursued by two of Amin's battalions.

Nyerere urged the Organization of African Unity to condemn Amin and more generally to enforce negative sanctions not only against colonial and racist regimes but also against "African fascists." OAU weakly recommended another cease fire. This advice was ignored, as Nyerere had already decided to chastise the Ugandans. Unilateral action proved necessary; with the exceptions of the frontline states, Ethiopia, and Madagascar, no other African government was willing even to censure Amin.

Assisted by about 900 Ugandan exiles, a quickly mobilized Tanzanian army had driven Ugandan troops from Kagera by mid-December of 1978. In January 1979, 10,000 soldiers of the People's Defence Force, reinforced by 30,000 members of the paramilitary People's Militia, invaded southern Uganda. The original objective was merely to punish the Ugandan forces, which had retreated to their barracks at Mbarara and Masaka. Perhaps because of the dangers posed by Libyan intervention on the side of Amin and the presence of long-range Soviet artillery that threatened the Tanzanian army, Nyerere decided quickly to push forward, take Kampala, and end the Amin scourge once and for all. On April 12, 1979, Tanzania recognized the interim government of former Makerere University Vice-Chancellor Yusuf Lule.

The war of Ugandan liberation cost Tanzania approximately Shs.10 million ($1.25 million) per day[15] and deprived the country of badly needed fuel, transport, food, and other essentials. Foreign exchange reserves dropped by three-quarters between November 1978 and April 1979 as the government sought to finance the operation. In spite of these sacrifices, Tanzania received scant praise from other African states; indeed, Kenya complained that the invasion was in violation of the OAU and UN charters.[16] The OAU asked Nyerere to withdraw his troops from Uganda, but he decided to leave as many as 26,000 men in the country for up to two years. Uganda helped pay for these security forces, but their presence raised the cost to Tanzania of the Ugandan campaign to about Shs.4 billion ($500 million) by 1980. The occupation was considered necessary in order to preserve the interim coalition government, but Dar es Salaam's custodial relationship with Kampala failed to produce this effect.

The Lule government, an unstable alliance of nationalist and communal groups, was replaced soon after it had taken office. The new regime was headed by Godfrey Binaisa, who was originally considered to be in closer sympathy with the Tanzanian presence if not with the political aspirations of former President Obote. Under increasing criticism within and outside Uganda, Tanzanian troops remained to ensure public order at least until the first post-Amin election of December 1980.

Interim President Binaisa quickly moved to solidify his leadership position by attempting to eliminate Milton Obote as a potential presidential contender. In doing so he alienated Obote's supporters in Uganda and the Tanzanians as well. Binaisa was summarily dismissed in May 1980, clearing the way for Obote's return to power. Obote was elected to the Ugandan presidency in a poll that was punctuated by charges and countercharges of vote rigging and coercion. This election solved nothing, as widespread acts of private and official violence ushered in the first year of the new regime. Tanzanian troops remained in the country, confronting an explosive situation that had already consumed a huge quantity of scarce developmental resources in the effort to reestablish peace and transnational rapport between Tanzania and its northwestern neighbor.

Tanzania and Kenya. In addition to maintaining the common services developed under the EAHC and EACSO, the East African Community initially sought to increase the rewards of regional economic cooperation. The EAC managed to improve the international marketing position of its members by concluding reciprocal trade agreements with the European Economic Community in

1969 and again in 1972. From these auspicious beginnings, EAC's fortunes steadily declined in the 1970s.

Kenya and Tanzania finally put an end to the community in 1977, but its days were already numbered in 1971. In that year Idi Amin accused Tanzania of trying to invade Uganda, closed his southern border, and suspended telephone and airline services between the two countries. Border clashes followed between Tanzanian and Ugandan troops. Even though he detested the Amin regime, President Nyerere offered concessions in an attempt to save the community. He agreed to accept Ugandan nominations to EAC posts and suspended a Tanzanian boycott of EAC meetings that had been in effect since the coup. Unmoved, Amin refused to sign EAC's 1971-1972 appropriations bill.[17] This decision effectively removed Uganda from the EAC and forestalled further action on the membership applications of Zambia, Ethiopia, Somalia, and Burundi. Had these countries been admitted to the community, they might have provided the EAC with the necessary momentum to survive and flourish.

The coup de grâce was administered by Kenya and Tanzania, which had been close political allies in the independence struggle but later evolved quite different developmental ideologies and economic strategies. In contrast to Tanzania's attempt to move toward an egalitarian and self-reliant agrarian socialism, Kenya followed a capitalist pattern of unbalanced economic growth, with heavy emphasis on foreign investment and industrial development. Kenyan President Jomo Kenyatta was an economic realist and an unapologetic materialist who shared few economic values with the idealistic and abstentious Julius Nyerere. Beyond these differences, Tanzanians feared that Kenya's material successes could lead to heightened local demands for similar amenities; and Kenyan leaders suspected that Tanzania's radical socialism and antielitism might become rallying points for domestic ethnic groups that were receiving fewer rewards and opportunities than were enjoyed by the dominant Kikuyu.

Bilateral economic relations first broke down in 1974, when Tanzania temporarily closed its border with Kenya in protest against heavily laden Kenyan trucks that were damaging Tanzania's few paved roads. Having already impounded three Tanzanian ferry boats in a dispute over railway maintenance costs, in January 1977 Kenya complained that it was being forced to carry most of the financial burden for the entire community. Arguing that the East African Airways Corporation was defaulting on its debt to Kenyan banks, the government waited until most of the aircraft were in Nairobi and then grounded the airline. Tanzania retaliated by again closing the border and seizing Kenyan property in Tanzania. A series of confiscations and resident alien repatriations followed, culminating in the refusal by both countries to make their 1977-1978 financial contributions to the community. Without an operating budget for the coming fiscal year, the EAC collapsed on July 1, 1977.

From the Tanzanian point of view, the community failed because of its discriminatory trade imbalances and its failure to develop a joint industrial strategy that would enhance the value of Tanzanian exports. In 1976, Kenya had accumulated a Shs.303 million ($38 million) surplus in its trade with Tanzania.[18] On the issue of industrial development, the official Tanzanian press lamented that foreigners or even local capitalists with investments in Kenya should be allowed access to markets in Tanzania and Uganda without hindrance because that is how Kenya wants it. For that Kenya has no problems. A problem arises when Tanzania proposes an East African industrial strategy, one that would enable Kenya, Tanzania and Uganda to use the East African market for their mutual and national development![19]

President Kenyatta died in 1978. His successor, President Daniel Arap Moi, has not changed Kenyatta's domestic economic policies, but he has shown a willingness to reach an accommodation with Tanzania and Uganda. He came to Arusha at Nyerere's invitation on May 30, 1979, and the two leaders discussed the reopening of air links between their capitals and various ways to assist in the reconstruction of Uganda. In January 1980 all three presidents met for the first time in ten years. The meeting lasted only an hour and produced a minor agreement on airspace rights. In July President Nyerere indicated his desire to normalize relations with Kenya, but only if the frozen assets of the EAC were distributed in a more equitable manner and if Kenya eased its criticism of Tanzania's involvement in Uganda. The presidents met again in January 1981, but they have yet to arrive at a mutually acceptable strategy for cooperation.[20]

These overtures may or may not lead to a rebirth of the East African Community. Whether they do will depend on a successful balancing of national and regional interests. For Tanzania to be satisfied, the regional inequalities that have consistently prevented economic unification must be eliminated. In a way that has come to typify Tanzanian foreign policy, international options are evaluated and selected in terms of their compatibility with the three philosophical goals of equality, socialism, and self-reliance. It remains to be seen whether Tanzania's erstwhile partners, and especially the skeptical Kenyans, will accept the regional version of equality.

Tanzania and Its Other Neighbors. Except in the special cases of Mozambique and Zambia, Tanzania interactions with other eastern and central African countries have followed a pattern of episodic if not serious conflict. Tanzania and Malawi have become involved in several unresolved disputes concerning Malawi's dealings with South Africa, Tanzania's harboring of Malawians opposed to the rule of President Kamuzu Banda, and the demarcation of the boundary between the two countries (Tanzania claims that the border should run down the middle of Lake Malawi; Malawi defends its historical placement on the eastern shore of the lake). In 1972 President Nyerere censured the Burundian regime of Michael Micombero for its harsh treatment of the country's Hutu ethnic majority. Some of the persecutions allegedly spread into western Tanzania, where a large number of Hutu had taken refuge, and it was not until Burundi underwent a military coup in 1976 that peace was restored to the area. Tanzania is still burdened with about 60,000 Burundians and with more than 100,000 other refugees from Rwanda, Uganda, and southern Africa. Previously friendly relations with Zaire deteriorated in 1975, when Presidents Nyerere and Mobutu Sese Seko supported different factions in the Angolan war of independence.

In its dealings with Mozambique and Zambia, Tanzania has reached the zenith and nadir of its regional encounters outside the former East African

Community. Presidents Nyerere and Samora Machel have maintained a warm relationship that began in the Mozambican liberation struggle. Tanzania provided military assistance before and after independence and subsequently concluded a series of agreements with Mozambique that promised to draw their economies closer together. For its part, Mozambique helped rescue Tanzania from the collapse of the East African Airways Corporation by supplying aircraft and pilots to the fledgling Air Tanzania Corporation. In January 1981, Nyerere and Machel announced plans for the construction of a "Unity Bridge" across the Ruvuma River.

Once extremely close, Tanzanian-Zambian relations have become more circumspect in recent years. With the assistance of the People's Republic of China, the Tazara railroad was completed in 1975 from Dar es Salaam to the Zambian copper fields. The railroad was intended to open previously inaccessible areas of Tanzania to development and to afford Zambia reliable access to the sea. The link was economically important to both countries: Tanzania needed the freight revenues from Zambian copper trade, and Zambia required an alternative to the port of Beira, which was effectively closed to Zambian shipments by the Mozambican and Zimbabwean liberation struggles. Tazara immediately began to experience technical, managerial, and financial problems that produced a series of economic disputes between the two countries. These difficulties arose as Zambia closed its Rhodesian border following an escalation of the Zimbabwean independence conflict. Anxious to reclaim his southern African trade option, Zambian President Kenneth Kaunda reopened the border, and a political rift also opened between Tanzania and Zambia. Relations further cooled when the two presidents supported different plans for Zimbabwean independence and when the Zambian government expelled about a thousand Tanzanians in its 1978 campaign against smugglers, criminals, and illegal aliens.

Economic and political relations have improved somewhat between the two countries but have never regained their previous levels of mutual trust and cooperation. Tanzania and Zambia are again trading, but on a reduced scale because of several factors. These include high transportation costs to and from Dar es Salaam, seemingly endless technical and managerial problems on Tazara and at Dar port, and the availability once again of Beira. In 1979 Tanzania momentarily opened its border with Kenya, so that 18,000 tons of grain could be transshipped to relieve a drought-related food shortage in Zambia. Human tragedy rather than economic opportunity is chiefly responsible for Tanzania's reconciliation with its closest central African ally.

Regional problems continue to create domestic and international headaches for Tanzanian policymakers. The Tazara railway is not achieving financial solvency and cannot without the millions of shillings in Zambian revenues now going to Zimbabwe and Mozambique. Tanzania and Kenya are both suffering from their failure to reach an economic accommodation. Political turmoil in Uganda has persisted and has disrupted Tanzania's international prestige and domestic stability. The Tanzanian invasion was denounced at a 1979 summit meeting of the Organization of African Unity by a group of states that feared the precedent set by this approach to resolving internal disorders. Tanzania has not succeeded in bringing peace to Uganda, and this fact does not help to justify either the original incursion or the subsequent stationing of security forces in the country.

At home, one member of parliament and fourteen officials of the Chama cha Mapinduzi were expelled from the party in May 1980 for criticizing domestic economic policies and the expense of maintaining troops in Uganda.[21] The MP and a district party chairman were detained, as were thirty military officers who had complained about not receiving their personal allowances. More than a thousand other people were reportedly held in Dar es Salaam following a protest demonstration against economic conditions and the Ugandan operation. For all this, civil strife has become so intense in Uganda that a visiting team from the International Monetary Fund was prematurely recalled from the country in April 1981. It was generally recognized that an abrupt ending of the Tanzanian presence would only worsen the instability, endanger the government of Milton Obote, and encourage a return to the anarchic state that had prompted the Tanzanian intervention. On the other hand, pressures mounted during early 1981 for a complete withdrawal of the remaining forces, which numbered approximately ten thousand soldiers and consisted mainly of paramilitary militiamen. Repatriation presented its own security problems, requiring the troops' immediate disarmament and reintegration into the society. Both tasks were complicated by the personal weapons the recruits had accumulated and the heightened economic expectations they had developed in their years of military service. In spite of the risks involved, Tanzanian authorities opted to recover the Shs.40 million ($5 million) monthly cost of maintaining the occupation force, and most of the soldiers were removed from Uganda by July 1981.

The Tanzanian posture in eastern and central Africa can be described as determined and even realistic, but also politically and economically precarious. The same can be said of Tanzania's position in the wider international system.

THE POLITICS OF DEPENDENCE
AND NONALIGNMENT

In his famous tract on imperialism and capitalism, Lenin spoke not only of the imperial powers and their colonial possessions, but also of "the diverse forms of dependent countries which, politically, are formally independent, but in fact, are enmeshed in the net of financial and diplomatic dependence."[22] One need not accept the entire Marxist-Leninist ideology to recognize that, in economic terms, Tanzania is one of these countries. In spite of its dedication to national self-reliance, Tanzania remains heavily dependent on the caprices of its trade and aid partners. National interests may be determined in Dar es Salaam, but the pursuit of these interests is constrained by decisions taken in more powerful capitals.

Politically if not economically, Tanzania has been able to further Nyerere's personal commitment to national self-determination. Between 1967 and 1972, support for southern African liberation was extended to include emancipation movements elsewhere in the world. Tanzania was one of only a few African states to recognize the Biafran government that emerged during the Nigerian civil war. This action reflected Nyerere's judgment that eastern Nigeria constituted a separate Ibo nation and was entitled to its independence from the hostile western and northern regions. Nyerere's position was not shared by many other African leaders, several of whom were worried about the example an independent Biafra might set for their own ethnic populations. Proceeding from the same moral premise that justified its recognition of Biafra, Tanzania managed to offend both Western and socialist powers by also recognizing the Provisional Revolutionary Government of South Vietnam, acknowledging the legitimacy of Prince Sihanouk's Cambodian exile government, and condemning the 1968 Soviet invasion of Czechoslovakia.

Tanzania's greatest foreign policy accomplishment in the post-1967 period perhaps lies in the preservation of its political and economic nonalignment. In the early 1970s, one-third of all foreign aid came from the People's Republic of China. By the early 1980s, China had become a minor donor and the largest share of foreign assistance was being received from the World Bank and from smaller European nations, including Sweden, Norway, and the Netherlands. The party-government's ultimate policy objective is still to achieve national economic independence. Its more immediate goal is to interact as widely as possible in the international arena and thereby minimize the influence of those nations upon whose help it must indefinitely depend. Tanzanians have experienced mixed results in their efforts to attain even this degree of autonomy.

Openings to the East

Tanzania has reached what it considers to be a reasonable if financially limited accommodation with the socialist states of Eastern Europe, Latin America, and Asia. Most important, the country has avoided any serious entanglement in the Sino-Soviet dispute—at least since the middle 1960s when Zanzibari foreign policies were painfully realigned to reflect the priorities of the new union. A particularly close friendship has been formed since the mid-1960s with the People's Republic of China. More recently, Tanzania has entered into an almost equally cordial relationship with Soviet-backed Cuba. The Cubans have built three agricultural schools since 1976 and have supplied fifty-two doctors to help improve rural medical practice. A 1978 agreement extended bilateral assistance to other areas of scientific and technical cooperation and included a scholarship program for Tanzanian students in Cuba. China has been willing to provide a wide range of financial and technical services on terms defined by Tanzania without many of the political and economic strings usually attached to foreign aid. In addition to outright grants, interest-free loans have been negotiated that are repayable through reciprocal trade in Chinese and Tanzanian goods. Only under such liberal arrangements could Tanzania afford the large and expensive Tazara project, and the Chinese have not demanded in return that Tanzania support their anti-Soviet foreign policy positions.[23]

In a manner typical of its approach to industrial countries in general, Tanzania has maintained a polite but somewhat distant relationship with the Soviet Union and its Eastern European satellites. The Tanzanian alliance with China has annoyed the Brezhnev government, which in turn offended the Tanzanians by supplying arms and military advisers to Amin's Uganda. Soviet military involvement in Uganda continued even after President Nikolai Podgorny paid an official visit to Tanzania in 1977 and was terminated only after Ugandan troops invaded Kagera in October 1978. The Soviets and East Germans, who had been influential in Zanzibar, have offered very little developmental assistance since the Tanzanian opening to China.

Although Tanzania receives about 60 percent of its military aid from the Soviet Union[24] and has applauded Soviet and Cuban military support for southern African liberation, the party-government clearly prefers to deal with socialist states that face developmental problems similar to its own. During an official visit to China in 1968, President Nyerere remarked:

> China and Tanzania have both declared themselves to be dedicated to the building of socialism. We have adopted different methods—if you like, we use different bricks and a different ground plan in the building of our people's societies. But by methods which seem to the peoples of our respective societies to be appropriate to their own needs, China and Tanzania are, I believe, working for the same objectives—the sovereignty of the people, and their freedom from exploitation.[25]

Nyerere has never established an equivalent unity of purpose with the Soviet Union and the other industrialized socialist states. The major problem with assistance from all socialist countries lies not in its unwanted political implications, however, but rather in its quantity. In 1980, communist governments met only about 10 percent of Tanzania's developmental aid requirements. Prime Minister Sokoine and Chinese Vice-Chairman Li Xiannian exchanged official visits in 1978 and 1979, but these and more recent contacts have not yet significantly increased the level of Chinese economic and technical assistance to Tanzania.

Openings to the West

Partly on the basis of its colonial experiences with Britain, the Tanzanian political leadership has traditionally had an ambivalent attitude toward the large industrial democracies. While admiring the popular representativeness of the Western systems of government and their strict adherence to the domestic rule of law, Tanzanians have also felt the economic exploitation, cultural denigration, and outright political oppression of which these systems are capable in their relations with smaller and weaker societies. Still, whatever goodwill Tanzanian elites harbor toward the great powers of the Northern Hemisphere is reserved largely for the West. Julius Nyerere illustrated this forbearance in an amusing aside during his first press conference after the Arusha Declaration was proclaimed.

> My friends the Americans have a knack of making themselves extremely unpopular, and sometimes it's due to clumsiness and sometimes it's due to bigness. If you are big, you are big, and if you are big you will be unpopular, you know. China is big. It has the problem of bigness. The United States is big. It has its problems of bigness. At one time the United Kingdom dominated the world. But they are very clever, the British. They have a sense of superiority, you know; they can take the problem of bigness. [Laughter.] If you hurl a brick at them, the British seem to say, "Well, we are so big if

you hurl a brick it is bound to fall on some British gentleman somewhere." The Americans haven't learned this. This blessed responsibility was thrust upon them . . . while they were growing up. The Americans are very human, they want to be loved. They want to be loved like all of us, and then they find that they don't get the love that they expect.[26]

Although Tanzania continues to receive nearly half its developmental assistance from the Western powers, it prefers to hold them at arm's length and to collaborate more intimately with multilateral development agencies and with smaller and less powerful states, such as Canada, the Netherlands, and the Scandinavian countries. The bulk of Tanzania's remaining foreign aid is drawn from these sources.

Tanzanian-American relations became severely strained in 1974 and again in 1975 when President Nyerere condemned Washington's growing interest in the Indian Ocean area and then refused to participate in negotiations concerning the release of three Americans kidnapped from Tanzania by Zairean rebels. He also reprimanded the United States for its covert role in Angola's postcolonial revolution and instructed his UN delegation to help initiate a General Assembly debate on the question of Puerto Rican independence.

Secretary of State Kissinger visited Dar es Salaam in 1976 and expressed his administration's desire to help achieve a peaceful transition to majority rule in Rhodesia. Kissinger's diplomacy eased tensions between the two countries, as did later U.S. efforts to achieve Namibian independence. President Nyerere visited Washington in 1977 and quickly reached a meeting of minds with President Carter on the issues of human rights and southern African liberation. Bilateral relations were further improved as the Carter administration began to focus U.S. developmental assistance on famine prevention and increased food production in the "poorest of the poor" developing countries. Responding to this new emphasis in U.S. development policy, President Nyerere requested a renewal of the Peace Corps program in Tanzania. (The Peace Corps had been expelled in 1972, partly because of its alleged infiltration by U.S. intelligence agents.)

Tanzania is likely to experience another period of difficulties with the United States. The Reagan administration will probably make a series of annual cuts in aid to Tanzania, reflecting a basic reorientation in U.S. Africa policy toward an overwhelming concern with national security and access to scarce natural resources. Repeal of the Clark Amendment (a 1976 congressional prohibition on U.S. intervention in Marxist and petroleum-rich Angola) is being considered, and Washington seems determined to continue building U.S. defensive capabilities in the Indian Ocean area, to increase its military assistance to strategically important countries like Sudan, Somalia, and Kenya, to reach some kind of rapprochement with the Republic of South Africa, and possibly to use food as a weapon in pursuit of these goals. For Tanzania, 1981 was a year of serious grain shortages. In its congressional food aid proposals for fiscal year 1982, the Reagan administration cut nearly $4 million from the $13.2 million previously planned for Tanzania.[27] President Nyerere has also gone on record as opposing each of the objectives to which Washington is now committed. For example, military delegations from the United States and four other NATO countries met in Paris during June 1980 and discussed the possibilities of joint military aid to selected African states. Nyerere reacted predictably to their communiqué. "It is the height of arrogance for anyone else [except the Organization of African Unity] to talk of establishing a pan-African force to defend Africa. It is quite obvious, moreover, that those who have put forward this idea and those who seek to initiate such a force are not interested in the freedom of Africa. They are interested in the domination of Africa."[28]

These are harsh words coming from a country that was compelled by drought to import more than 100,000 tons of U.S. food grains in 1980 and 1981. The relationship with the United States epitomizes both sides of Tanzania's role in the contemporary international system, one grounded in an unhappy mixture of uncompromising political leadership and unavoidable economic subservience. This same pattern emerges in the country's relations with other Western powers. Nyerere has consistently criticized France for selling arms to South Africa. Ties with Britain were all but severed in 1965 over the British refusal to force a withdrawal of Rhodesia's unilateral declaration of independence. The British Foreign Office was itself aroused in 1971 and 1972 when Tanzania confiscated nearly Shs.40 million ($6 million) in British-owned property. Having already terminated its own assistance to Tanzania, Britain retaliated by vetoing a World Bank loan for the development of Tanzanian tea production. In 1974 Britain resumed its bilateral aid program, and Tanzania has expressed some satisfaction with post-1976 British support for southern African liberation. In September 1978, however, Tanzania nationalized the operations and assets of Lonrho, a British multinational corporation that was accused of breaking international economic sanctions against Rhodesia and interfering with the Zimbabwean liberation forces. Lonrho demanded $54 million in compensation but later agreed to a Tanzanian settlement of less than $2 million. This episode did little to enhance Tanzania's popularity in London.

Bargaining from a position of moral strength but practical weakness, Tanzanians look out upon an increasingly hostile international environment. The greenest oasis in this otherwise forbidding landscape is found in the friendship and unqualified generosity of the Scandinavian countries. These states have an ideological affinity with Tanzania and are willing to help finance its quest for equality, democracy, and socialism. More than 30 percent of Tanzania's annual economic assistance is contributed by Sweden, Norway, Denmark, and Finland. Yet because of their growing need for financial aid, Tanzanian policymakers must not only encourage their friends but also work with powerful and unpredictable governments that tend to pursue less unselfish interests in countries like Tanzania. As they reflect on the demands of their assignments, these leaders must frequently recall a disturbingly appropriate African proverb: "When the elephants fight, it is the grass which gets trampled."

7

Assessing the Tanzanian Experiment

TANZANIA: MODEL OF SUCCESS OR LESSON IN FAILURE?

Tanzania has been subjected to both conservative and radical criticism. Rightists castigate the continuous and seemingly disjointed social experimentation that has characterized the Tanzanian experiment in democratic socialism. They also inveigh against the party-government's occasional lapses into a kind of unpremeditated authoritarianism, the negative effects of which are supposedly aggravated by its unpredictability. Finally, conservative observers point to the country's worsening economic situation and blame much of it on the widespread collectivization of production and reward distribution. Such policies as enforced villagization, universal price and wage controls, and the comprehensive nationalization of major economic activities are alleged to have destroyed private incentives, discouraged much-needed foreign investment, and rendered Tanzanians incapable of accommodating their rapidly growing population through technically and economically feasible improvements in productivity.

The Tanzanian experiment has been no less strenuously attacked from the opposite ideological pole. Marxists and neo-Marxists maintain that the country provides textbook examples of economic dependency and periphery capitalism. To them, political independence and social transformation mean little in the context of the colonial economic relationship that still prevails and determines the quality of Tanzanian life. Leftists point out that African peasants continue to produce primary agricultural products, which are exported to industrial countries in return for imported commodities, which are mostly consumed by the governing elite and by an emergent class of wage earners and relatively prosperous cash-crop farmers. In spite of a successful campaign to curtail luxury imports, the only qualitative change acknowledged to have occurred since independence involves a shift in the major beneficiaries of the international dependency relationship. The British and their Asian retainers are said to have been replaced by a privileged group of party-government officials.

Critics on the left hold that elitism and class formation are reinforced by the party-government's recent encouragement of small-scale capitalism, which not only increases the country's addiction to imported factors of production but also further widens the income gap between urban workers and subsistence farmers. Although foreign investment has been limited in the interests of maximizing national self-reliance, foreign aid has grown in importance and is argued to have systematically biased the political and decision-making processes. Observing that many aspects of the 1972 decentralization campaign were recommended by a U.S. consulting firm, the radical critique maintains that decentralization has created regional cadres of self-seeking elites. These local power brokers are blamed for weakening party discipline and preventing the conversion of the Chama cha Mapinduzi from a loose-knit mass movement into the type of tightly structured vanguard party that the radicals view as necessary for a complete transition to socialism. The decentralization policy is also accused of having turned the central government ministries into operationally meaningless organizations whose essential function is merely to attract donor funds. Foreign aid is often accompanied by formally and informally mandated guidelines on how it should be used.[1] If such influences are sufficiently strong and pervasive—and leftist critics fear that they are—one may fairly question the reality of Tanzanian independence.

Attacks from the right and left notwithstanding, certain facts cannot be ignored. Tanzanians *are* more equal than are their counterparts in countries like Zambia and Kenya.[2] Governmental stability *is* greater in Tanzania than in such ethnically competitive societies as Zaire and Uganda. Political repression *is* felt less here than in dictatorships like Malawi's. Measured in terms of education and health care, the quality of life *has* improved more in Tanzania than in any of these other countries.[3]

Tanzania has been hailed as one of Africa's most hopeful models of socially and politically responsible development. Understandably, most of the credit for this achievement is reserved for Julius Nyerere and his unwillingness to accept the more decisive but elitist and coercive "solutions" of both right-wing and left-wing developmental strategies.

> Although profoundly committed to an egalitarian society, he has witnessed developments that would seem to lessen the likelihood of Tanzania's achieving such an objective. Nevertheless he has remained committed to democratic participation as an essential feature of Tanzania's lengthy transition to socialism. His belief in democracy has persisted. He has recurringly refused to allow himself or his government to become so certain of their own integrity, of the validity of their vision and the adequacy of their means as to feel that extensive coercion is justified. This is, perhaps, the characteristic of Tanzanian socialism which explains more than any other the international interest which it has attracted.[4]

Dostoyevsky once said that ideas tend to have their consequences. The consequences of Julius Nyerere's political ideas have generated such a storm of controversy that it is scarcely possible to find a dispassionate commentary on the modern Tanzanian scene. Nevertheless, it is important to attempt an assessment of the Tanzanian experiment and to speculate on the directions in which it may lead the country in the difficult years to come.

The Experiment at Twenty Years

In spite of its many domestic and international problems, Tanzania is a remarkably stable country. Public order is maintained through the management of tensions in an egalitarian and politically well-organized society rather than through the patrimonial elitism and systematic suppression of dissident opinions that prevail in many less developed countries. Recent evidence of the Tanzanian approach is not hard to find. In February 1978 President Nyerere helped to celebrate the first anniversary of the Chama cha Mapinduzi by releasing more than 7,000 petty criminals and twenty-six political detainees. In March he expelled 367 university students, including his own child, for protesting modest increases in the salaries of politicians. By June, 346 of the students had been reinstated. Zanzibari officials drafted a new constitution in 1979, which for the first time requires their government to be elected.

The party is particularly concerned with the problem of obtaining greater popular support. The CCM National Executive Committee met in secret in May 1980 to discuss such issues as alleged police brutality, authoritarian tendencies among local party-government cadres, and the possibility of eliminating the detention law. According to informal reports, this meeting was convened because of mass political and economic alienation, poor production, and officials who were considered unresponsive to the needs of the people.

Economically related political disaffection still exists in Tanzania, and there are no easy solutions to this problem. Elections under the new Zanzibari constitution produced the desired effect—the selection of younger and more flexible representatives who oppose Zanzibar's separatist tradition and favor closer integration with the mainland. Sixteen old-guard leaders were detained in June 1980 following the disclosure of a plot to overthrow the government. The detainees had argued against a closer relationship with mainland Tanzania, which they held responsible for the recent deterioration of Zanzibar's once-thriving agricultural economy. This charge is not entirely unfounded. Tanzania must now spend approximately 60 percent of its export earnings on imported petroleum products. Lacking a reasonable tax base, the party-government commands few domestic financial resources with which to stimulate productivity, maintain its high level of welfare investment, and at the same time strive toward national economic independence.

The social and political effects of this predicament are becoming increasingly obvious. In his study of public investments between 1964 and 1973, Clark concluded that "because of the extremely rural nature of the society today it will be at least twenty to thirty years before the country is significantly altered in this respect. For this reason a strategy which ignores the rural sector ignores most of the population."[5] Since 1973, most rural dwellers have been physically uprooted and relocated but have not been provided with the necessary financial incentives and technical assistance for them to restore, let along exceed, their previous levels of production. As a result, more and more peasants are withdrawing from the governmentally sponsored cash economy, and legally marketed food output has fallen to about 90 percent of its 1969-1971 average. Rural dwellers are preoccupied with their own survival; they are also reproducing at an unprecedented rate and contributing a flood of unemployable migrants to the already over-crowded and economically distressed cities.

In response to its immediate financial crisis, the party-government has been forced to request more aid and also to emphasize local earnings at the expense of welfare investments and the equalization of incomes. By 1981 Tanzania was receiving more per capita international assistance than any other tropical African country, and almost 70 percent of all new development was funded from foreign loans and grants. In an effort to reduce the foreign debt, an increasing amount of money is now being committed to import-substituting and basic industries. But in-dustrial development can also contribute to a deterioration in the rural-urban terms of trade, encourage higher rates of urban migration and unemployment, and exacerbate political alienation and economic withdrawal in the rural areas. At the level of the party branch and local development committee, popular discon-tent was more widespread in the early 1980s than at any other time since in-dependence. It will not dissipate if present economic trends persist. This loss of support, unless it is checked, will nullify the hard-won gains in socioeconomic equality, human welfare, and mass political participation and will destroy all hope for an eventual transition to democratic socialism.

The Tanzanian experiment is not yet finished, but it cannot succeed through the rigid application of any single ideological formula, including Nyerere's. Pragmatically selected policies are required that foster productivity and an appropriate balancing of investment and consumption without sacrificing the larger goal of an equitable and democratically integrated social order. Steering this partly uncharted course will be complicated by growing bureaucratic inefficiency and corruption, by the impending departure of President Nyerere from active public life, and not least, by Tanzania's uncertain international position.

Tanzania's domestic predicament is clearly related to its peripheral role in the international political and economic systems. Life at the periphery will become even more precarious as the industrial states adjust their foreign policies to com-pensate for their own international insecurities and domestic economic reversals. Tanzania's ideological orientation allows no compromise with economic and military intervention in the affairs of Africa. Yet Tanzanian policymakers must also come to grips with the realities of their dependence on imported materials, skills, money, and now food. The suppliers of these resources are capable, if only inadvertently, of disrupting recipient governments and preventing their coopera-tion with other Third World states. It is certain, for example, that Tanzanian-Kenyan relations will be further strained if the United States proceeds with its intended eight-fold increase in military assistance to Kenya as part of the Reagan administration's plan to strengthen U.S. influence in northeastern Africa, the Indian Ocean, and the Persian Gulf region.

Of the many perils confronting Tanzania in the international arena, none is as serious and yet as manageable as the danger of food dependency. A recent warning to the poorest countries of the southern hemisphere applies directly and immediately to Tanzania.

> The South . . . needs to make an effort at achieving self-sufficiency in food. Faulty strategies of development, in which the agricultural sector has been discriminated

against in urban-rural trade relations, have obliged many countries which once enjoyed a food surplus to import grain and other foodstuffs. The effect has been to make
the Third World dependent on the U.S. and a few other countries for its food. With
the Reagan Administration set to pursue a hard line *macho* policy in its foreign relations, the Third World runs the risk of a food blackmail by the U.S.[6]

Creativity, energy, and discipline will be needed to reduce the impact of
hostile foreign policies and to avert the related tragedies of mass hunger and social
disintegration. The immediate challenge lies not on the diplomatic circuit,
however, but in the newly created villages. Consolidation of the rural population
may well be a necessary condition for the self-help improvements that form the
core of Tanzania's developmental strategy. Unless it is accompanied by effective
measures to stimulate these improvements, the proliferation of densely settled
villages will only exacerbate a number of existing ecological hazards and threaten
not just future development, but human survival itself. These dangers include the
spread of human and animal disease; the destruction of agricultural land, especially in semiarid zones, because of overcropping and insufficient time allowed for
soil regeneration; localized depletions of potable water, fuelwood, and construction materials; and increasing desertification caused by the overgrazing of
livestock on marginal grasslands.[7] If rural dwellers are compelled to live in essentially unassisted villages, what were once serious but manageable problems will
quickly become major crises. With the meager resources at their disposal to avoid
these catastrophes and prevent civil strife in the rural and urban areas, Tanzanians run the risk of being diverted from their original experiment in political and
economic development.

THE CRITICAL YEARS AHEAD

Poor and weak, Tanzania lacks the developmental options open to more
generously endowed developing countries. This unfortunate fact places a great
burden on the political leadership. If it is to achieve economic independence,
maintain political stability, and create a permanently well-integrated and
democratic social order, the party-government must adhere to the literal meaning
of its slogan *ujamaa na kujitegemea*—that is, it must work toward the more efficient
mobilization and equal sharing of locally available resources. This will require that
a much larger share of development capital be extracted from the society. Further
advances toward socialism and self-reliance will also necessitate sharp reductions
in human capital expenditures for all sectors of the society, even stricter curtail-
ment of imported petrochemical consumption, and prolonged adherence to a
policy of subsistence-level wages and farm incomes. The future of Tanzania will be
determined largely by whether its top political leadership can accomplish the formidable task of obtaining elite and mass support without also providing the
material rewards both groups expect.

Tanzania is one of the last African countries about which this speculation
can still be entertained. As Michael Bratton has pointed out, political stability on
most of the continent depends on two factors: "First, the magnitude of patronage
resources available to the center and, second, the extent to which local leaders are

able to use patronage to prevent the hardening of peasant disaffections into the consciousness of a permanently excluded social class."[8] If the Chama cha Mapinduzi allows itself to fall into a patrimonial mode of operation, it will be found wanting on both conditions for stability. The CCM has shown a tendency to reward its officials financially and to develop local bailiwicks of semiautonomous party strength. Unless these trends are halted, given the CCM's limited ability to buy political support, the party could lapse into an unstable patronage system lacking the capacity to satisfy all the claimants who increasingly hold it hostage.

Tanzania's future depends not only on the interactions of the political center with its local periphery, but also on the attitudes and behavior of its educated bureaucratic elites. The Tanzanian policy system emphasizes equality in place of opportunities for individual advancement. Yet unbending adherence to this austere strategy can lead technicians and administrators to believe that they are not being adequately compensated for their skills and efforts. In this situation, the elites could revolt and attempt to create a system in which individual economic opportunities are stressed. Because of Tanzania's domestic poverty, this option too must fail unless the public sector is willing to sacrifice its freedom of action on behalf of a policy line that encourages indiscriminate foreign investment and private accumulations of wealth and power. As with the patrimonial scenario, the choice of this strategy would quickly put an end to the present experiment in democratic socialism.

Tanzania faces two other possibilities. Under mounting ecological and economic pressures, the political system could degenerate into a series of anarchic power struggles similar to those that have befallen Uganda. In response to these confrontations—or perhaps to prevent them from happening—the existing party-government could be replaced by the military, a military-bureaucratic coalition, or even a militarily supported vanguard party. That the country has shown little propensity to move in any of these directions can be attributed to the moderating influence of President Nyerere. On the other hand, Nyerere will soon leave public life, and it is not yet clear whether his authority can be effectively passed to a successor. Like all new states, Tanzania will reach its final formula for stability and development when it has institutionalized its formula for political leadership.

The experiment of the past twenty years is being put to its ultimate test in the third decade of Tanzanian independence. Julius Nyerere has given his people the opportunity to work toward a democratic and humane future. In light of what the future might instead hold in store, Tanzanians have no choice other than to proceed with their experiment in the principled and yet realistic manner of its founder. Above all else, the present leadership generation must pay heed to Nyerere's haunting admonition: "While other countries aim to reach the moon, we must aim to reach the villages."

Notes

INTRODUCTION

1. Following the Zanzibari revolution of January 1964, Tanganyika and Zanzibar merged to form the United Republic of Tanzania. In this study, Tanzania will be identified by its present short name when both Tanganyika and Zanzibar are considered. In discussions of Tanganyika that are not historically specific, the term "mainland Tanzania" will be used. Zanzibar and the adjoining island of Pemba will be collectively referred to as "Zanzibar."

CHAPTER 1. THE ORIGINS OF TANZANIA

1. Richard E. Leakey and Roger Lewin, *People of the Lake: Mankind and Its Beginnings* (New York: Avon Books, 1979), Chapter 5; and Sonia Cole, *The Prehistory of East Africa* (New York: Mentor Books, 1963), Chapters 4 and 5.
2. See Roland Oliver, "The East African Interior," in Roland Oliver (ed.), *The Cambridge History of Africa*, Vol. 3 (Cambridge: Cambridge University Press, 1977), pp. 621–69.
3. See Irving Kaplan, "Historical Setting," in Irving Kaplan (ed.), *Tanzania: A Country Study* (Washington: American University, 1978), pp. 16–31; and Edward A. Alpers, "The Coast and the Development of the Caravan Trade," in I. N. Kimambo and A. J. Temu (eds.), *A History of Tanzania* (Nairobi: East African Publishing House, 1969), pp. 35–56.
4. A.H.J. Prins, *The Swahili-Speaking Peoples of Zanzibar and the East African Coast* (London: International African Institute, 1961), p. 42.
5. See John Iliffe, *Tanganyika Under German Rule, 1905–1912* (Cambridge: Cambridge University Press, 1969); and R. F. Eberlie, "The German Achievement in East Africa," *Tanganyika Notes and Records* 55 (September 1960), pp. 181–214.
6. Kaplan, "Historical Setting," p. 40.
7. For informative accounts of this remarkable campaign, see Leonard Mosley, *Duel for Kilimanjaro: An Account of the East African Campaign, 1914–1918* (London: Weidenfeld and Nicolson, 1963); and Charles Miller, *Battle for the Bundu: The First World War in East Africa* (New York: Macmillan, 1974).
8. League of Nations, *British Mandate for East Africa*, C.449 (I) & M. 345 (a), 1922, VI, cited in B.T.G. Chidzero, *Tanganyika and International Trusteeship* (London: Oxford University Press, 1961), p. 259.
9. J. Clagett Taylor, *The Political Development of Tanganyika* (Stanford, Calif.:

Stanford University Press, 1963), p. 26. For further reading on the origins of eastern Africa's Asian community, see D. P. Ghai (ed.), *Portrait of a Minority: The Asians of East Africa* (Nairobi: Oxford University Press, 1965), Chapter 1.

10. Donald Cameron, "Principles of Native Administration and Their Application," *Local Government Memoranda: No. 1* (Dar es Salaam: Government Printer, 1930), p. 1.

11. Tanganyika, *Native Authority: An Ordinance to Prescribe the Powers and Duties of Native Authorities*, Chap. 72 of the Laws of Tanganyika (1927).

12. See J. Gus Liebenow, "The Legitimacy of Alien Relationship: The Nyaturu of Tanganyika," *Western Political Quarterly* 14 (March 1961), pp. 64–86.

13. Tanganyika, Secretariat Files, 23866 (African Associations: Government Policy Towards), General Minute from His Excellency the Governor [Sir Harold MacMichael], June 26, 1936.

14. Quoted in Ralph Austen, *Political Generations in Bukoba: 1890–1939* (Kampala: East African Institute of Social Research, Makerere University, 1963), p. 14.

15. See Michael F. Lofchie, *Zanzibar: Background to Revolution* (Princeton, N.J.: Princeton University Press, 1965), pp. 69–95 and 99–126.

16. For accounts of the famous Groundnut Scheme and Meru Land Case, see Chidzero, *Tanganyika and International Trusteeship*, pp. 234–245.

17. Tanganyika, *Development Plan for Tanganyika, 1961/62–1963/64* (Dar es Salaam: Government Printer, 1962). See also International Bank for Reconstruction and Development (World Bank), *The Economic Development of Tanganyika* (Baltimore: Johns Hopkins Press, 1961).

18. Murray Lunan, "Lecture to the Tanganyika Society on Some Changes in Tanganyika Agriculture in the Past Twenty Years," Dar es Salaam, 1964, p. 3.

19. Tanganyika, Ministry of Local Government and Housing, *Annual Report of the Social Development Division, 1960* (Dar es Salaam: Government Printer, 1961), p. 3.

20. For a detailed analysis of one such episode in the Uluguru Mountains of eastern Tanzania, see Roland Young and Henry Fosbrooke, *Land and Politics Among the Luguru of Tanganyika* (London: Routledge and Kegan Paul, 1960).

21. Tanganyika, *Development Plan, 1961/62–1963/64*, p. 8.

22. Tanganyika, Secretariat Files, 23866, Communication from the Secretary General of the Tanganyika African Association to the Member for Law and Order, April 27, 1950.

23. Ibid., Memorandum to All Provincial Commissioners from the Chief Secretary, No. LG 12/017 of November 28, 1956.

24. Quoted in Kaplan, "Historical Setting," p. 56.

25. Lofchie, *Zanzibar*, p. 178.

CHAPTER 2. THE ECOLOGY OF CHANGE

1. Amir Jamal, *The Critical Phase of Emergent African States* (Nairobi: East African Publishing House, 1965), p. 5.

2. Ibid.

3. Hans Ruthenberg, *Agricultural Development in Tanganyika* (Berlin: Springer-Verlag, 1964), pp. 8–10.

4. United Nations Fund for Population Activities, *Tanzania: Report of Mission on Needs Assessment for Population Assistance* (New York: United Nations Fund for Population Activities, 1979), pp. 1 and 8; and World Bank, *World Development Report, 1981* (New York: Oxford University Press, 1981), p. 134.

5. World Bank, *World Development Report, 1981*, p. 168.

6. Replacement-level fertility is achieved when the average number of female births equals the average number of female deaths in a child-bearing population. The World Bank projects the attainment of replacement-level fertility in Tanzania by the year 2035 and a stationary population by 2100. A stationary population is reached when the total birthrate equals the total death rate, with the population's age structure remaining constant. The hypothetical size of Tanzania's stationary population is 97 million. Ibid., p. 166.

7. Tanzania, *1978 Population Census Preliminary Report* (Dar es Salaam: Bureau of Statistics, Ministry of Finance and Planning, n.d.), pp. 178–180.

8. *Daily News* (Dar es Salaam), January 17, 1979.

9. Richard E. Stren, *Urban Inequality and Housing Policy in Tanzania: The Problem of Squatting* (Berkeley: Institute of International Studies, University of California, 1975), pp. 24–25.

10. See International Bank for Reconstruction and Development (World Bank), *Tanzania: Basic Economic Report* (Washington: IBRD, 1977), p. 23; and International Labour Office, *Towards Self-Reliance: Development, Employment and Equity Issues in Tanzania* (Addis Ababa: ILO Jobs and Skills Programme for Africa, 1978), passim.

11. See Roland Oliver, *The Missionary Factor in East Africa* (London: Longman, 1952), for a classic account of missionary influences in Tanzania.

12. See B. L. Hall, *Adult Education and the Development of Socialism in Tanzania* (Nairobi: East African Literature Bureau, 1976).

13. See I. D. Resnick (ed.), *Tanzania: Revolution by Education* (London: Longman, 1968); and H. Hinzen and V. H. Hundsdorfer (eds.), *Education for Liberation and Development: The Tanzanian Experience* (Hamburg: UNESCO Institute for Education, 1979).

14. See Marjorie J. Mbilinyi, "The New Woman and Traditional Norms in Tanzania," *Journal of Modern African Studies* 10 (1972), pp. 57–72.

15. See J. Gus Liebenow, *Colonial Rule and Political Development in Tanzania: The Case of the Makonde* (Evanston, Ill.: Northwestern University Press, 1971).

16. See Sally Falk Moore and Paul Puritt, *The Chagga and Meru of Tanzania* (London: International African Institute, 1977).

17. See Brian Taylor, "The Western Lacustrine Bantu," in Daryll Forde (ed.), *Ethnographic Survey of Africa, Vol. 3, East Central Africa* (London: International African Institute, 1962).

18. See R. G. Abrahams, *The Political Organization of Unyamwezi* (Cambridge: Cambridge University Press, 1967).

19. The following analysis draws heavily from data reported in World Bank, *World Development Report, 1981*. See Chapter 5 for a fuller analysis of the Tanzanian economy and economic policy system.

20. U.S. Department of Agriculture, *Food Problems and Prospects in Sub-Saharan Africa: The Decade of the 1980s* (Washington, D.C.: Economic Research Service, USDA, August 1980), p. 192.

21. This concern was debated in the Tanzanian press during 1970. The various arguments are reproduced in I. G. Shivji (ed.), *Tourism and Socialist Development* (Dar es Salaam: Tanzania Publishing House, 1975).

22. For an analysis of these supernatural belief systems in contemporary eastern Africa, see John Middleton and E. H. Winter, *Witchcraft and Sorcery in East Africa* (New York: Praeger Publishers, 1963).

23. Tanganyika, *President's Address to the National Assembly, 10th December, 1962* (Dar es Salaam: Tanganyika Information Services, Ministry of Information and Tourism, n.d.), pp. 17–18.

CHAPTER 3. THE AMBIGUITIES OF INDEPENDENCE

1. Cranford Pratt, *The Critical Phase in Tanzania, 1945–1968* (Cambridge: Cambridge University Press, 1976), pp. 90–114.

2. Tanganyika, *Development Plan for Tanganyika, 1961/62–1963/64* (Dar es Salaam: Government Printer, 1962).

3. Pratt, *Critical Phase in Tanzania*, p. 91.

4. Ibid., pp. 93–94.

5. Julius K. Nyerere, "Africanization of the Civil Service," excerpted from a speech before parliament of October 19, 1960, and reprinted in Nyerere, *Freedom and Unity: Uhuru na Umoja* (Dar es Salaam: Oxford University Press, 1966), p. 100.

6. *Ujamaa—The Basis of African Socialism* (Dar es Salaam: Tanganyika Standard, 1962), reprinted in Nyerere, *Freedom and Unity*, pp. 162–171; *The Second Scramble* (Dar es Salaam: Tanganyika Standard, 1962), further developed into a speech before the Afro-Asian Solidarity Conference of February 4, 1963, and excerpted in Nyerere, *Freedom and Unity*, pp. 204–208; *TANU na Raia* [TANU and the people] (Dar es Salaam: Tanganyika African National Union Press, 1962); and *Tujisahihishe* [Let us correct our mistakes] (Dar es Salaam: Tanganyika African National Union Press, 1962).

7. Nyerere, "Introduction," in *Freedom and Unity*, p. 10.

8. Ibid., p. 11.

9. Nyerere, "Individual Human Rights," excerpted from an opening address to the Pan-African Freedom Movement of East and Central Africa Conference of September 1959 in ibid., p. 70. Also quoted in Pratt, *Critical Phase in Tanzania*, p. 64.

10. Nyerere, *Second Scramble*, p. 207.

11. Nyerere, "Responsible Self-Government Proposals," excerpted from a speech before parliament of December 16, 1959, in Nyerere, *Freedom and Unity*, pp. 77–78. Also quoted in Pratt, *Critical Phase in Tanzania*, pp. 65–66.

12. (Dar es Salaam: Tanganyika Standard Ltd., n.d.); also excerpted in Nyerere, *Freedom and Unity*, pp. 195–203.

13. See, for example, "One-Party Government," *Spearhead* 1 (November 1961), pp. 7–10.

14. Nyerere, *Democracy and the Party System*, p. 1.

15. Ibid., p. 15.

16. Ibid., p. 25.

17. Ibid., p. 26.

18. Nyerere, *Ujamaa*, p. 162.

19. Ibid., p. 164.

20. Cf. Pratt, *Critical Phase in Tanzania*, pp. 72–77.

21. Nyerere, quoted in the *Times* (London), January 23, 1962.

22. Tanzania, *Budget Survey, 1964–65* (Dar es Salaam: Government Printer, 1964), p. 9, cited in Pratt, *Critical Phase in Tanzania*, p. 124.

23. See Tanganyika, *High-Level Manpower Requirements and Resources in Tanganyika, 1962–1967*, prepared by George Tobias, Consultant to the Government of Tanganyika from the Ford Foundation (Dar es Salaam: Government Printer, 1963). This investigation followed two unpublished reports, prepared in 1960 and 1961 by Ford Foundation representatives J. L. Thurston and J. Donald Kingsley. Like the Tobias report, these studies were aimed at finding ways quickly to Africanize the civil service without seriously disrupting efficiency.

24. Tanganyika, *Africanisation of the Civil Service, Annual Report, 1963* (Dar es Salaam: Government Printer, 1964), p. 2.

25. Pratt, *Critical Phase in Tanzania*, p.126.

26. Julius Nyerere, "To Plan Is to Choose," excerpted from a speech before the TANU National Conference, May 28, 1969, in Nyerere, *Freedom and Development: Uhuru na Maendeleo* (New York: Oxford University Press, 1973), p. 84.

27. The following studies provide insights into these local political innovations: Goran Hyden, *Political Development in Rural Tanzania: TANU Yajenga Nchi* (Nairobi: East African Publishing House, 1969); Clyde Ingle, "The Ten-House Cell System in Tanzania: A Consideration of an Emerging Village Institution," *Journal of Developing Areas* 6 (January 1972), pp. 211–225; Clyde Ingle, *From Village to State in Tanzania* (Ithaca, N.Y.: Cornell University Press, 1972); Norman N. Miller, "The Rural African Party: Political Participation in Tanzania," *American Political Science Review* 64 (June 1970), pp. 548–571; Jean F. O'Barr, "Cell Leaders in Tanzania," *African Studies Review* 15 (December 1972), pp. 437–465; and Rodger Yeager, "Micropolitics and Transformation: A Tanzania Study of Political Interaction and Institutionalization," Ph.D. dissertation, Syracuse University, 1968, pp. 123–132.

28. Tanzania, *Statistical Abstract, 1965* (Dar es Salaam: Government Printer, 1967), p. 146.

29. For more detailed analyses of the village settlement policy, see Yeager, "Micropolitics," pp. 135–167; and Yeager, "Micropolitical Dimensions of Development and National Integration in Rural Africa: Concepts and an Application," *African Studies Review* 15 (December 1972), pp. 367–402.

30. Tanganyika, *An Act to Establish a Rural Settlement Commission and for Matters Incidental Thereto*, Act No. 62 of 1963 (Dar es Salaam: Government Printer, 1964).

31. Tanganyika and Zanzibar, *Five-Year Plan for Economic and Social Development, 1st July, 1964–30th June, 1969, Vol. I, General Analysis* (Dar es Salaam: Government Printer, 1964), pp. ix–x and 19–21.

32. Julius Nyerere, *President's Address to the National Assembly, Thursday, 6th June, 1965* (Dar es Salaam: Mwananchi Publishing Company, n.d.), p. 5.

33. Tanzania, *Address by the Second Vice President Mr. R. M. Kawawa, at The Opening of the Rural Development Planning Seminar at the University College, Dar es Salaam, on Monday, April 4, 1966* (Dar es Salaam: Tanzania Information Services, 1966), p. 4.

34. Tanzania, *Report of the Presidential Commission on the Establishment of a Democratic One Party State* (Dar es Salaam: Government Printer, 1965). Nyerere delayed in appointing the commission because of the possibility that an East African Federation, then under discussion with Kenya and Uganda, might be created and have to be taken into account in any constitutional changes. The discussions produced little agreement among the three countries, and Nyerere decided to proceed with his efforts to create a democratic one-party state.

35. Tanzania, *Proposals of the Tanzania Government for the Establishment of a Democratic One-Party State*, Government Paper No. 1 of 1965 (Dar es Salaam: Government Printer, 1965).

36. Tanzania, *An Act to Declare the Interim Constitution of Tanzania*, Act No. 43 of 1965 (Dar es Salaam: Government Printer, 1965).

37. For the definitive analysis of this election, see Lionel Cliffe (ed.), *One Party Democracy: The 1965 Tanzania General Elections* (Nairobi: East African Publishing House, 1967). Also see Henry Bienen, *Tanzania: Party Transformation and Economic Development* (Princeton, N.J.: Princeton University Press, 1970), pp. 382–405.

38. Tanzania, *An Act to Confer Upon the National Executive Committee of the Party the Like Privileges Relating to the Summoning of Witnesses, the Taking of Evidence and the Production of Documents as Are Enjoyed by the National Assembly*, Act No. 49 of 1965 (Dar es Salaam: Government Printer, 1965).

39. For detailed critiques of these trends, see A. Van de Laar, "Growth and Income

Distribution in Tanzania Since Independence," in Lionel Cliffe and John S. Saul (eds.), *Socialism in Tanzania: An Interdisciplinary Reader, Vol. 1, Politics* (Nairobi: East African Publishing House, 1972), pp. 106–117; and Justinian Rweyemamu, *Underdevelopment and Industrialization in Tanzania* (Nairobi: Oxford University Press, 1973), pp. 46–57. In an expression of frustration with the rising elite generation, in 1966 Nyerere temporarily expelled 393 students from the University of Dar es Salaam. They had protested a policy requiring them to serve the country for a time following graduation, at a fraction of their future salaries. Most of these students were enrolled under government scholarships.

40. Nyerere, *Second Scramble*, p. 205.

41. Tanzania, *Statistical Abstract, 1965*, p. 109.

42. Julius K. Nyerere, "Hotuba ya Rais Nyerere Kuhusu Mwungano" [Speech of President Nyerere concerning the union], reproduced in Tanzania, *Muungano wa Tanganyika na Unguja* [The union of Tanganyika and Zanzibar] (Dar es Salaam: Tanganyika Information Services, 1964), p. 4.

CHAPTER 4. TOWARD SOCIALISM AND DEMOCRACY

1. Reginald Herbold Green, "Tanzanian Political Economy Goals, Strategies, and Results, 1967–74: Notes Towards an Interim Assessment," in Bismarck U. Mwansasu and Cranford Pratt (eds.), *Towards Socialism in Tanzania* (Toronto: University of Toronto Press, 1979), p. 22.

2. Julius K. Nyerere, "The Arusha Declaration," in Nyerere, *Ujamaa: Essays on Socialism* (New York: Oxford University Press, 1968), p. 28. This version of the declaration incorporates several revisions that Nyerere made to clarify ambiguities in an earlier English translation from the original Kiswahili.

3. Ibid., p. 33. Emphasis in original.

4. For critiques of the Arusha Declaration for failing to adopt this position, see K. Ngombale-Mwiru, "The Arusha Declaration on Ujamaa na Kujitegemea and the Perspectives for Building Socialism on Tanzania" and "The Policy of Self-Reliance," in Lionel Cliffe and John S. Saul (eds.), *Socialism in Tanzania: An Interdisciplinary Reader, Vol. 2, Policies* (Nairobi: East African Publishing House, 1973), pp. 52–61 and 66–70.

5. Nyerere, "Arusha Declaration," p. 36.

6. For a commentary on this tendency among members of parliament, see Helge Kjekshus, "Parliament in a One-Party State – The Bunge of Tanzania," *Journal of Modern African Studies* 12 (March 1974), pp. 35–37.

7. Joel Samoff, *Tanzania: Local Politics and the Structure of Power* (Madison: University of Wisconsin Press, 1974), p. 156.

8. These large-scale nationalizations were followed by a massive takeover of small retail shops, termed Operesheni Maduka (Operation Shops). Operesheni Maduka is further discussed in this chapter.

9. Julius K. Nyerere, "Decentralization," in Nyerere, *Freedom and Development: Uhuru na Maendeleo* (New York: Oxford University Press, 1973), p. 344.

10. Tanzania, *The Decentralisation of Government Administration Act of 1972* (Dar es Salaam: Government Printer, 1972).

11. For analyses and critiques of the 1970 election, see Election Study Committee, University of Dar es Salaam, *Socialism and Participation: Tanzania's 1970 National Elections* (Dar es Salaam: Tanzania Publishing House, 1974).

12. Michael F. Lofchie, "Agrarian Crisis and Economic Liberalisation in Tanzania," *Journal of Modern African Studies* 19 (1978), p. 451.

13. For a similar conclusion, see ibid.

14. Tanzania, *An Act to Provide for the Registration of Villages, the Administration of Registered Villages and Designation of Ujamaa Villages*, Act No. 12 of 1975 (Dar es Salaam: Government Printer, 1975).

15. In this context, "operations" were defined as compulsory movements of entire local populations into villages. See Dean E. McHenry, Jr., *Tanzania's Ujamaa Villages: The Implementation of a Rural Development Strategy* (Berkeley: Institute of International Studies, University of California, 1979), p. 133. Before and after compulsion was introduced, an undetermined number of existing communities were included in the villagization statistics, even though these were traditional villages whose residence patterns had been rationalized to conform with the official conception of properly organized settlements.

16. Compiled and extrapolated from data reproduced in ibid., Chapter 5; Adolpho Mascarenhas, "After Villagization—What?" in Mwansasu and Pratt, *Towards Socialism in Tanzania*, pp. 152–156; and Tanzania, *1978 Population Census Preliminary Report* (Dar es Salaam: Bureau of Statistics, Ministry of Finance and Planning, n.d.), p. 176. These figures deal exclusively with the mainland. Zanzibar was not included in Operation Tanzania.

17. Mascarenhas, "After Villagization," pp. 153–154.

18. Ibid., p. 156.

19. *Daily News* (Dar es Salaam), November 18, 1976.

20. TANU Regional Secretary Joseph Rwegasira, quoted in ibid., November 4, 1977.

21. Lofchie, "Agrarian Crisis," p. 452.

22. Jean M. Due, *Costs, Returns and Repayment Experiences of Ujamaa Villages in Tanzania, 1973–1976* (Washington, D.C.: University Press of America, 1980), p. 9. These declines were caused not only by villagization but also by the disastrous droughts that plagued Tanzania between 1973 and 1975.

23. Lofchie, "Agrarian Crisis," p. 456.

24. See Colin Legum (ed.), *Africa Contemporary Record: Annual Survey and Documents, 1976-1977*, Vol. 9 (London: Rex Collings, 1977), pp. B347–348.

25. Joel Samoff, review of McHenry, *Tanzania's Ujamaa Villages*, in *American Political Science Review* 74 (December 1980), p. 1121.

26. Julius K. Nyerere, *The Arusha Declaration—Ten Years After* (Dar es Salaam: Government Printer, 1977). See also *10 Years of Arusha* (Dar es Salaam: Tanganyika Standard [Newspapers], 1977).

27. Tanzania, President's Office, "An Official Reply to Africa Confidential Article of July 16, 1980" (Washington: Embassy of the United Republic of Tanzania, mimeo., n.d.).

28. Nyerere, *Arusha Declaration—Ten Years After*, p. 33. The Politics is Agriculture (*Siasa ni Kilimo*) campaign urged party-government officials to spend part of their time in the villages in order to provide technical and organizational assistance and gain a deeper appreciation of problems confronting the villagers. Some leaders responded by joining *ujamaa* villages, notably the president's younger brother Joseph, who had served as a regional commissioner. Most officials ignored the call until village residence was later required for local technical personnel and even central government officers.

29. Legum, *Africa Contemporary Record, 1976-1977*, p. B341.

30. For an official account of the CCM's creation and first year of life, see Ali A. Mohamed, *Kuzaliwa kwa Chama Cha Mapinduzi* [Birth of the Revolutionary party] (Dar es Salaam: Tanzania Publishing House, 1979).

31. CCM Constitution, Preamble, reproduced in *10 Years of Arusha*, p. 49.

32. Cf. ibid., Articles 3 and 4, pp. 51–63; and Tanganyika African National Union, *Sheria na Madhumuni ya Chama* [Law and purpose of the party] (Dar es Salaam: Mwananchi Publishing Co., n.d.), pp. 4–21.

33. *Daily News*, September 21, 1977.

34. Colin Legum (ed.), *Africa Contemporary Record: Annual Survey and Documents, 1977-1978*, Vol. 10 (New York: Africana Publishing Company, 1979), p. B405.

35. Nyerere, *Arusha Declaration—Ten Years After*, p. 39.

36. *Daily News*, January 21, 1981.

37. Ibid., September 27, 1980.

38. Under the party and government constitutions, the CCM National Conference selects a single candidate for the presidency, who is then approved or rejected by the voters.

39. *Daily News*, October 30, 1980. Jumbe's plurality was in excess of 96 percent. As head of the Zanzibar government, and because the presidency was occupied by a mainlander, Jumbe automatically became vice-president of Tanzania.

40. Ibid., January 1, 16, and 24, 1981.

CHAPTER 5. TOWARD SOCIALISM AND SELF-RELIANCE

1. For a summary of these projects, see Tanganyika and Zanzibar, *Five-Year Plan for Economic and Social Development, 1st July, 1964–30th June, 1969, Vol. 2, The Programmes* (Dar es Salaam: Government Printer, 1964), pp. 145-151.

2. Ibid., Vol. 1, *General Analysis*, p. xiii.

3. Tanzania, *The Economic Survey, 1973-74* (Dar es Salaam: National Printing Co., 1975), p. 6. It should be noted that the first plan's long-term social and infrastructural goals have largely been achieved. The Tanzanian per capita income stood at about Shs.392 ($56) in 1964, and the goal was to have it reach Shs.900 ($129) by 1980. At Shs.2,080 ($260), the present per capita income far exceeds this target. The plan also aimed toward self-reliance in trained manpower by 1980 and an increase in Tanzanians' average life expectancy from thirty-five to fifty years. Although still understaffed, key public sector agencies are now staffed almost entirely by Tanzanians. The average life expectancy has risen to approximately fifty-two years.

4. Colin Leys, Cranford Pratt, and Brian van Arkadie have provided critical analyses of the first five-year plan in Cliffe and Saul, *Socialism in Tanzania*, Vol. 2, *Policies*, pp. 5–39.

5. W. Arthur Lewis, *The Evolution of the International Economic Order* (Princeton, N.J.: Princeton University Press, 1978), p. 37.

6. Tanzania, *Second Five-Year Plan for Economic and Social Development, 1st July, 1969–30th June, 1974, Vol. 1, General Analysis* (Dar es Salaam: Government Printer, 1969), p. 27.

7. Tanzania, *Second Five-Year Plan, Vol. 2, The Programmes*, p. 13.

8. See ibid., Vol. 3, *Regional Perspectives*, and Vol. 4, *Survey of the High and Middle Manpower Requirements and Resources*.

9. Tanzania, *The Economic Survey, 1977-78* (Dar es Salaam: Government Printer, 1979), p. 11.

10. Kaplan, *Tanzania*, p. 192.

11. Tanzania, *Economic Survey, 1973-74*, p. 57; and Tanzania, *Economic Survey, 1977-78*, p. 50.

12. Tanzania, *Economic Survey, 1973-74*, p. 76; and *Economic Survey, 1977-78*, p. 79.

13. Cf. Cranford Pratt. "Tanzania's Transition to Socialism: Reflections of a Democratic Socialist," in Mwansasu and Pratt, *Towards Socialism in Tanzania*, p. 202; and Ann Seidman, "Some Comments on Planning in East Africa," in Cliffe and Saul, *Socialism in Tanzania*, Vol. 2, *Policies*, pp. 84–87.

14. Reginald Herbold Green, "Tanzanian Political Economy Goals, Strategies, and

Results, 1967-74: Notes Towards an Interim Assessment," in Mwansasu and Pratt, *Towards Socialism in Tanzania*, p. 24.

15. Tanzania, *Third Five Year Plan for Economic and Social Development, 1st July, 1976-30th June, 1981*, Volume 1, Part 1, *General Perspectives* (Dar es Salaam: National Printing Co., n.d.), p. 54; and Kaplan, *Tanzania*, pp. 285-286.

16. By this time, the value of Tanzania's currency was fluctuating between seven and eight shillings to the U.S. dollar. Following currency devaluations in 1975 and 1979, by 1981 the ratio stood at slightly more than eight to one. In order to facilitate meaningful economic comparisons for the contemporary period, a conversion factor of eight to one is applied to all post-1974 financial data.

17. Between 1975 and 1977 Tanzania accumulated a negative trade balance of Shs.2.15 billion ($269 million) and an international payments deficit of Shs.1.1 billion ($137 million). Tanzania, *Economic Survey, 1977-78*, pp. 18 and 24.

18. Legum, *Africa Contemporary Record, 1976-1977*, p. B356.

19. Ibid., pp. B354-356.

20. Tanzania, *Economic Survey, 1977-78*, p. 11.

21. Tanzania, *Third Five Year Plan*, Volume 1, p. 5.

22. World Bank, *World Development Report, 1980* (New York: Oxford University Press, 1980), pp. 110, 112, 116, and 152.

23. Ibid., pp. 134 and 138.

24. Pius Msekwa, "The Quest for Workers' Participation in Tanzania," in N.S.K. Tumbo et al., *Labour in Tanzania* (Dar es Salaam: Tanzania Publishing House, 1977), p. 81.

25. Nyerere, quoted in *New African*, August 1978, p. 20.

26. *Daily News*, January 22 and 24, 1981.

27. *Financial Times* (London), October 30, 1980, cited in *Africa Report* 26 (January-February 1981), p. 32.

28. *Daily News*, February 5, 1981.

29. Ibid., January 17, 1981.

30. Gerald K. Helleiner, "Aid and Dependence in Africa: Issues for Recipients," in Timothy M. Shaw and Kenneth A. Heard (eds.), *The Politics of Africa: Dependence and Development* (New York: Africana Publishing Company, 1979), p. 226.

31. International Labour Office, *Towards Self-Reliance*, p. xx.

32. Julius K. Nyerere, "Ten Years After Independence," reprinted in Nyerere, *Freedom and Development*, p. 333.

33. Pratt, "Tanzania's Transition to Socialism," p. 215.

34. Norman N. Miller, "Food in Tanzania: Policy, Equity and Distribution," paper presented at the American Universities Field Staff Conference on the Politics of Food, Hanover, N.H., November 1980, p. 17.

35. See Goran Hyden, *Beyond Ujamaa in Tanzania: Underdevelopment and an Uncaptured Peasantry* (Berkeley: University of California Press, 1980).

36. Miller, "Food in Tanzania," p. 19.

37. In its global assessment for mid-1980, the UN World Food Council estimated that about 2 million Tanzanians then faced life-threatening food shortages.

CHAPTER 6. INTERNATIONAL LEADERSHIP AND DEPENDENCE

1. Julius K. Nyerere, "Stability and Change in Africa," in Nyerere, *Man and Development: Binadamu na Maendeleo* (New York: Oxford University Press, 1974), p. 49.

2. Julius K. Nyerere, "Developing Tasks of Non-Alignment," in ibid., pp. 67–68.

3. Ibid., pp. 77–78.

4. For an analysis of the formation and early activities of the OAU, see Zdenek Červenka, *The Organization of African Unity and Its Charter* (New York: Praeger Publishers, 1969). For a more recent account, see Michael Wolfers, *Politics in the Organization of African Unity* (New York: Methuen, 1976).

5. Okwudiba Nnoli, *Self Reliance and Foreign Policy in Tanzania* (New York: NOK Publishers, 1978), p. 255.

6. The U.S. House of Representatives conducted an extensive investigation of these interests in the early 1970s. For a record of this inquiry, see U.S. Congress, House, Committee on Foreign Affairs, Subcommittee on Africa, *Hearings: U.S. Business Involvement in Southern Africa*, three parts, 92nd and 93rd Cong., 1st Sess., 1972 and 1973.

7. About 1,500 soldiers were involved in this operation. This number represents a sizable commitment of troops, given that Tanzania's armed forces totaled only about 14,600 men and women in 1976. See Legum, *Africa Contemporary Record, 1976–1977*, pp. B352–353.

8. *Daily News*, November 12, 1976, quoted in ibid., p. B360.

9. These parties included the front-line states of Tanzania, Mozambique, Zambia, Angola, and Botswana, in addition to Britain, the United States, South Africa, the Rhodesian minority regime, and the competing nationalist groups. Tanzania was instrumental in unifying the two most powerful of these independence movements. At a June 1977 meeting of front-line states in Luanda, Angola, President Nyerere persuaded the Zimbabwe African People's Union of Joshua Nkomo and the Zimbabwe African National Union of Robert Mugabe to form the Patriotic Front. The front-line states then vowed their unqualified support for this alliance.

10. For a concise historical overview of regional cooperation in eastern Africa, see Anthony J. Hughes, *East Africa: The Search for Unity* (Harmondsworth: Penguin Books, 1963), especially pp. 213–264.

11. Cf. Adekunle Ajala, *Pan-Africanism: Evolution, Progress and Prospects* (New York: St. Martin's Press, 1974), pp. 40–43.

12. See Julius K. Nyerere, "East African Federation," in Nyerere, *Freedom and Unity*, pp. 85–98.

13. Tanganyika and Zanzibar Information Service, *Kampala Agreement* (Dar es Salaam: Mwananchi Publishing Co., 1964).

14. See Norman N. Miller, "East Africa's New Decade of Doubt, Part I: Kenya and Tanzania," and "East Africa's New Decade of Doubt, Part II: Uganda and Regional Perspectives," *American Universities Field Staff Reports*, 1980/9 and 1980/12 (Hanover, N.H.: American Universities Field Staff, 1980).

15. Legum, *Africa Contemporary Record, 1978-1979*, p. B397.

16. This criticism is particularly odd in light of the fact that Amin had also threatened military action against Kenya and at one point laid claim to one-third of Kenya's territory in the western part of the country. The Kenyan position is also strange in that it continued to be expressed for some time after Amin was overthrown. This not only annoyed the Tanzanians but also threatened to alienate the new Ugandan government, with which Kenya was best advised to make its peace.

17. For further analysis of these difficulties, see Donald Rothchild and Robert L. Curry, Jr., *Scarcity, Choice, and Public Policy in Middle Africa* (Berkeley: University of California Press, 1978), pp. 236–241.

18. Central Bank of Kenya, *Economic and Financial Review*, Vol. 3 (1977), cited in *New African Development* (London), March 1978, p. 59.

19. *Daily News*, quoted in ibid., February 1977, p. 122.

20. The January 1981 meeting took place in Kampala and was attended by presidents Nyerere, Moi, and Obote, in addition to President Kaunda of Zambia. The discussions produced one significant result; the establishment of an authority to supervise the distribution of the former East African Community's assets once an acceptable apportionment formula is devised.

. 21. *Times* (London), May 24, 1980, cited in *Africa Report* 25 (July-August 1980), p. 25.

22. V. I. Lenin, *Imperialism, The Highest Stage of Capitalism* (Moscow: Foreign Languages Publishing House, n.d.), p. 144.

23. Tanzania favored the Popular Movement for the Liberation of Angola (MPLA), which defeated the National Union for the Total Independence of Angola (UNITA) in the final struggle for control of the Angolan government. Tanzanian-Chinese relations were not affected by the fact that the Soviet Union and Cuba materially assisted the MPLA while China endorsed UNITA.

24. In the aftermath of the January 1964 army mutiny, Nigerian troops were quickly called in to replace the British Marines who had put down the rebellion. Following the departure of the Nigerians in the fall of 1964, Tanzania solicited military assistance from several countries, including Canada, the People's Republic of China, Israel, and the Federal Republic of Germany. During this period China, the German Democratic Republic, and the Soviet Union engaged in military training activities on Zanzibar. Since 1969, most foreign military aid has been supplied by the Soviet Union and, to a lesser extent, China. For further information on the Tanzanian armed forces and their sources of support, see Kaplan, *Tanzania*, pp. 240–257; and U.S. Arms Control and Disarmament Agency, *World Military Expenditures and Arms Transfers, 1969–1978* (Washington, D.C.: U.S. Arms Control and Disarmament Agency, December 1980), pp. 69, 153, and 161.

25. Julius K. Nyerere, "The Supremacy of the People," in Nyerere, *Freedom and Development*, p. 38.

26. President Nyerere's first press conference after the Arusha Declaration and the nationalization of industries, March 4, 1967 (taped and transcribed by Cranford Pratt). I am indebted to Professor John R. Nellis of Syracuse University for providing me with copies of Professor Pratt's tape and transcript.

27. U.S. Congress, House, Committee on Foreign Affairs, Subcommittee on Africa, *Hearings and Markup: Foreign Assistance Legislation for Fiscal Year 1982*, Part 8, 97th Cong., 1st Sess., 1981, p. 157.

28. *Africa Currents*, January 1979, quoted in Legum, *Africa Contemporary Record, 1978-1979*, p. A33. The official press echoed these sentiments in its commentary on the Reagan administration's announcement that it would seek repeal of the Clark Amendment, which bans U.S. interference in Angola. "There could hardly be a greater display of big-power arrogance . . . this plan is worse than the Soviet invasion of Afghanistan." *Sunday News* (Dar es Salaam), March 15, 1981.

CHAPTER 7. ASSESSING THE TANZANIAN EXPERIMENT

1. Michael F. Lofchie, "Agrarian Crisis," p. 456. As noted in Chapter 4, Lofchie was referring to the international pressures exerted on Tanzania to reemphasize agricultural production in the aftermath of the villagization program. The U.S. Agency for International Development (AID) has provided a more recent, albeit tentative, example of these attempted interventions in the Tanzanian policy process. The original draft of AID's 1982 Tanzanian strategy statement proposed to concentrate U.S. technical assistance in four of

the country's poorest regions. In my discussions with officials of the Ministry of Agriculture, I found no evidence that this emphasis reflected a central government priority for AID assistance. Although I understand that the strategy statement was subsequently modified, I have not been invited to read this revised edition. For the originally proposed strategy, see U.S. Agency for International Development, *Tanzania: Country Development Strategy Statement, FY 82* (Washington, D.C.: U.S. International Development Cooperation Agency, January 1980).

2. For useful analyses of Zambia and Kenya along these lines, see Michael Bratton, *The Local Politics of Rural Development: Peasant and Party-State in Zambia* (Hanover, N.H.: University Press of New England, 1980); and Colin Leys, *Underdevelopment in Kenya: The Political Economy of Neocolonialism, 1964–1971* (London: Heinemann, 1975).

3. In the combined areas of education and health, Tanzania's closest African rival is Kenya. The World Bank reported that by 1976, Tanzania had attained a 66 percent adult literacy rate; Kenya had achieved a 45 percent rate. With the exceptions of Liberia, Uganda, and Zimbabwe, by 1978 Kenya and Tanzania led the rest of tropical Africa in their populations' average life expectancy at birth. For these and related quality of life indicators, see World Bank, *World Development Report, 1981*, pp. 134, 176, and 178.

4. Pratt, *Critical Phase in Tanzania*, p. 263.

5. W. Edmund Clark, *Socialist Development and Public Investment in Tanzania, 1964–1973* (Toronto: University of Toronto Press, 1978), p. 243.

6. Denzil Peiris, "South-South Collaboration: A Strategy to Transcend Mutual Differences," *Third World Media* (London), December 19, 1980, quoted in *World Press Review* (New York), March 1981, p. 40.

7. Cf. Mascarenhas, "After Villagization," p. 158. Mascarenhas notes that in the country's preexisting ecological context, "Tanzanians adopted a settlement pattern of scattered homesteads as their most suitable defence. Unless the villagization programme actively works to change that context, scattered homesteads may remain, with good reason, a desirable pattern in the eyes of some Tanzanians." Ibid., p. 162.

8. Bratton, *Local Politics of Rural Development*, p. 270.

An Introductory Bibliography

The following scholarly and reference works provide additional information about Tanzania. These sources represent only a small sampling of the available literature on this important African country.

PREINDEPENDENCE HISTORY

Ayany, S. G. A History of Zanzibar. Nairobi: East African Literature Bureau, 1970.
    A brief but informative account of preindependence Zanzibar, focusing on the turbulent social, economic, and political events of the 1950s and early 1960s.
Kimambo, I. N., and Temu, A. J. (eds.). A History of Tanzania. Nairobi: East African Publishing House, 1969.
    An excellent collection of essays on the historical experiences of Tanzania from its initial settlement until the late 1960s. Includes chapters on prehistory, the caravan trade, precolonial and colonial politics, the rise of Tanganyikan nationalism, factors involved in the Zanzibari revolution, and the period from independence to the Arusha Declaration.
Taylor, J. Clagett. The Political Development of Tanganyika. Stanford, Calif.: Stanford University Press, 1963.
    A concise description of the mainland under British rule and of the local, territorial, and interterritorial developments that led to Tanganyikan independence.

SOCIETY AND CULTURE

Hinzen, H., and Hundsdorfer, V. H. (eds.). Education for Liberation and Development: The Tanzanian Experience. Hamburg: UNESCO Institute for Education, 1979.
    Examines the application of "lifelong" educational policies in Tanzania. Includes materials on curriculum development and evaluation, technical and adult education, and the integration of formal and informal educational programs.
Mbilinyi, Marjorie J. "The New Woman and Traditional Norms in Tanzania." Journal of Modern African Studies 10 (1972):57–72.
    Discusses the traditional roles of Tanzanian women, the impact of colonialism and modernization on these roles, and the obstacles to the further emancipation of Tanzania's "new women."
Prins, A.H.J. The Swahili-Speaking Peoples of Zanzibar and the East African Coast. London: International African Institute, 1961.

A definitive ethnographic survey of the Arab, Shirazi, and Swahili cultures. Includes information on the historical, socioeconomic, political, artistic, and religious aspects of these communities.

Wilson, Monica. *Good Company: A Study of Nyakyusa Age-Villages*. London: Oxford University Press, 1951.

Winans, Edgar G. *Shambala: The Constitution of a Traditional State*. London: Routledge and Kegan Paul, 1962.

Two excellent studies of politically decentralized (Nyakyusa) and centralized (Shambala) traditional societies, illustrating the rich cultural diversity of mainland Tanzania.

POLITICS AND GOVERNMENT

Bienen, Henry. *Tanzania: Party Transformation and Economic Development*. Princeton, N.J.: Princeton University Press, 1970.

A detailed analysis of the Tanganyika African National Union, including its role as an independence movement, its postindependence organization and ideology, and its participation in economic development programs. Concludes with a section on political problems encountered in Tanzania between 1964 and 1969.

Hopkins, Raymond F. *Political Roles in a New State: Tanzania's First Decade*. New Haven, Conn.: Yale University Press, 1971.

An interview-based investigation of the roles and role-expectations of Tanzanian administrative, legislative, and executive elites. Includes an evaluation of the relationship between political roles, stability, and democracy.

Hyden, Goran. *Political Development in Rural Tanzania: TANU Yajenga Nchi*. Nairobi: East African Publishing House, 1969.

An illuminating view of local political and developmental attitudes, based on research among the Haya people of western Tanzania.

Mwansasu, Bismarck U., and Pratt, Cranford (eds.). *Towards Socialism in Tanzania*. Toronto: University of Toronto Press, 1979.

A set of critical essays on Tanzania's attempt to develop socialism and self-reliance, emphasizing questions of developmental strategy, the performance of various party-government agencies, and the interim effects of villagization.

Pratt, Cranford. *The Critical Phase in Tanzania, 1945-1968*. Cambridge: Cambridge University Press, 1976.

A monumental study of Julius Nyerere and the emergence of modern Tanzania. Essential reading for anyone seeking to understand the full significance of Nyerere's ideas, actions, and influence in Tanzania and the world.

Samoff, Joel. *Tanzania: Local Politics and the Structure of Power*. Madison: University of Wisconsin Press, 1974.

A major case study of politics in Moshi, Kilimanjaro Region. Discusses key local issues and the leadership behavior of local party-government officials. Moshi's party organization and the politics of self-reliance are also examined.

MODERNIZATION AND DEVELOPMENT

Boesen, Jannik, et al. *Ujamaa: Socialism from Above*. New York: Holmes and Meier, 1978.

Studies on the application of *ujamaa* policy in West Lake Region. Topics include the developmental problems of the villages, villagization, the emergence of a local class structure, and the bureaucratization of *ujamaa* policy implementation.

Hyden, Goran. *Beyond Ujamaa in Tanzania: Underdevelopment and an Uncaptured Peasantry.* Berkeley: University of California Press, 1980.

A provocative analysis of rural development policies from the early colonial period to the present. Hyden argues that the deepest roots of Tanzania's developmental problems lie not in the international economic system but in an unimproved mode of agricultural production that provides no incentives for peasants to work toward a successful transformation of the domestic economy.

Kim, Kwan S., et al. (eds.). *Papers on the Political Economy of Tanzania.* Nairobi: Heinemann Educational Books, 1979.

An up-to-date collection of economic studies on the post–Arusha Declaration period. Includes information on economic planning, industrial and rural development, money and banking, international economic relations, and human resource investment.

McHenry, Dean E., Jr. *Tanzania's Ujamaa Villages: The Implementation of a Rural Development Strategy.* Berkeley: Institute of International Studies, University of California, 1979.

The most comprehensive study yet completed on *ujamaa* and villagization policy implementation, and on problems experienced in attempting to encourage villagers to work as well as live together in collective settlements.

Shivji, Issa G. *Class Struggles in Tanzania.* Dar es Salaam: Tanzania Publishing House, 1975.

An application of Marxist class analysis to Tanzania. Traces the rise of a "bureaucratic bourgeoisie" and seeks to identify the beginnings of political and economic class struggles in the rural and urban areas.

FOREIGN RELATIONS

Ajala, Adekunle. *Pan-Africanism: Evolution, Progress and Prospects.* New York: St. Martin's Press, 1974.

A detailed account of the successes and failures of pan-African political and economic movements, with references to the Tanzanian role in Africa's attempts to create supranational unity.

Nnoli, Okwudiba. *Self-Reliance and Foreign Policy in Tanzania.* New York: NOK Publishers, 1978.

A comprehensive review of Tanzanian foreign policy until the early 1970s. Discusses the diplomatic inertia of the early independence period and later policy formulations that still influence Tanzania's international position.

Nyerere, Julius K. *Crusade for Liberation.* Dar es Salaam: Oxford University Press, 1979.

A record of President Nyerere's 1977 visit to the United States in response to the first invitation extended by the Carter administration to an African head of state. Includes the texts of Nyerere's speeches and press interviews on important foreign policy issues, especially southern African liberation.

Rothchild, Donald, and Curry, Robert L., Jr. *Scarcity, Choice, and Public Policy in Middle Africa.* Berkeley: University of California Press, 1978.

Relates domestic to international goals, decision-making rules, and policy choices in tropical Africa's quest for development and economic independence. Includes references to Tanzania's developmental approaches, economic problems, and place in the international system.

REFERENCE WORKS

Kurtz, Laura S. *Historical Dictionary of Tanzania*. Metuchen, N.J.: Scarecrow Press, 1978.
A useful reference source, containing information on the political elites of
Tanganyika, Zanzibar, and Tanzania; a chronology of important events; a dictionary
of social, economic, and political topics; and an extensive bibliography.
Mwenegoha, H.A.K. *Mwalimu Julius Kambarage Nyerere: A Bio-Bibliography*. Nairobi: Foundation Books, 1976.
An exhaustive compilation of references to the writings of President Nyerere and to
commentaries on his political career and thought. An essential guide for readers
wishing to learn more about Africa's preeminent statesman and political philosopher.

Index

Abdul Rahman Mohammed, 22–23, 56
"Able man." *See Homo habilis*
African Liberation Committee, 95
African National Congress, 95
African National Union, 124(n9)
African People's Union of Rhodesia, 95
African unity, 94–104, 108, 124(n9),
    125(n20)
Afro-Asian Solidarity Conference, 55
Afro-Shirazi Party (ASP), 22–23, 52–53,
    54, 56, 73, 74, 75
Afro-Shirazi Union (ASU), 22
Agriculture, 26–27, 121(n28),
    125–126(n1)
  cash crops, 10, 37–38, 50, 51(Table
    3.1), 80, 81, 86, 89, 108
  food production, 26, 37, 69, 80, 81,
    82, 86, 89, 91, 107
  socialistic, 60
AID. *See* United States Agency for
    International Development
Amin, Idi, 2, 99–100, 101, 105, 124(n16)
Anglo-Zanzibari treaty, 8
Angola, 96, 107, 124(n9), 125(n28)
Arab Association, 15, 21–22
Arusha Declaration, 59–61, 63, 70–73,
    75, 77, 80, 82, 85, 88, 89, 95, 106
  leadership code, 60–61, 77, 78
Askari, 11
ASP. *See* Afro-Shirazi Party
ASU. *See* Afro-Shirazi Union

Babu. *See* Abdul Rahman Mohammed
Baganda Society, 99
Bahaya Union. *See* Bukoba Bahaya
    Union

Balance-of-payments, 38, 87
Balance of trade, 82
Banda, Kamuzu, 102
Barghash (Sultan of Zanzibar), 9
Belgium, 12
Biafra, 104
Binaisa, Godfrey, 100
Birth rates, 27–28, 117(n6)
Bismark, Otto von, 9
Botswana, 96, 124(n9)
Bratton, Michael, 113
Brezhnev, Leonid, 105
Bukoba Bahaya Union, 15, 18
Burundi, 9, 101

Cambodia, 105
Cameron, Sir Donald, 12–13, 14
Canada, 57, 107, 125(n24)
Carter, Jimmy, 107
CCM. *See* Chama cha Mapinduzi
Chagga, 14, 18, 36, 37, 50
Chama cha Mapinduzi (CCM), 2, 35,
    73, 74–76, 87, 104, 110, 111, 114,
    122(n38)
China. *See* People's Republic of China
Christianity, 34
Cities. *See* Urban centers
Clark, W. Edmund, 111
Clark Amendment (U.S.), 107, 125(n28)
Climate, 2, 26–27, 30, 31(Fig. 2.2),
    32–33(Table 2.3), 65, 68
Clutton-Brock, Guy, 45
Coastal strip, 7–9
Colonial period, 8–21
Common Man's Charter, 99
Congo. *See* Zaire

131

DATE DUE
